FIFTY SOUTH

The Wreck of the Dundonald

BY

MARGARET BEAMES

Rangitawa
PUBLISHING

Fifty South first published 2014

Published by Rangitawa Publishing, Feilding, New Zealand.

www.rangitawapublishing.com

rangitawa@xtra.co.nz

ISBN 978-0-9941088-3-8

For my brother John.

Also by Margaret Beames.

Pumpkin Pie

The Greenstone Summer

Hidden Valley

The Parkhurst Boys

Clown Magic

The Girl in Blue

The Glass Tower

Archway Arrow

Storm

Outlanders

Rabbit

The Singing Cave

Josef's Bear

Spirit of the Deep

Duster

Oliver in the Garden

Oliver's Party

Oliver Goes Exploring

The Mouse That Danced

Illustrations

Cover Four masted barque *Dundonald* Wikipedia image.

Pages 73, 74, 76, 77, 79.

Lithographs by Ernest Prater.

H.Escott-Inman *"The Castaways of Disappointment Island."*

Published by S.W. Partridge & Co. 1911

(Personal property of M.Beames.)

Page 75.

Sealskin slippers made by the crew of the *Dundonald.* Canterbury Museum, Christchurch (Photo by M.Beames.)

Page 78.

Members of the *Dundonald* crew with the coracle frame. Canterbury Museum Christchurch. (Photo by M.Beames,)

Page 80.

The crew of the *Dundonald* Canterbury Museum, Christchurch.

(Photo by M.Beames)

Page 81

Members of the *Dundonald* crew aboard the *Hinemoa.*

By permission of the Alexander Turnbull Library, National Library of New Zealand.

Page 82

Display of photographs taken by E.A.Phillips of Phillips Brothers, relating to the wreck of the *Dundonald* in 1907.

By permission of the Alexander Turnbull Library, national Library of New Zealand.

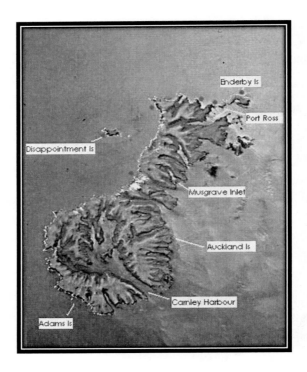

The Auckland Islands

CHAPTER ONE

On 7 March 1907 a four-masted barque smashed into the streaming black cliffs of a tiny island in the icy waters of the sub-Antarctic – and that might have been the end for all on board, but in fact it was just the beginning of an extraordinary adventure.

My interest in the story began when my brother gave me a book, a rather shabby, old-fashioned looking book, published some hundred years before. "I thought you might like this," he said. I looked at it doubtfully – *The Castaways of Disappointment Island* it was called, by Rev. H. Escott-Inman – and put it aside for a few days, but one evening I opened the covers and started reading and found myself hooked by the castaways' story, *being an account of their sufferings* as the sub-title of the book declared, told to the author by one of the survivors, Charles Eyre.

Charlie Eyre had always wanted to be a sailor. He was a London lad, born within the sound of Bow Bells, I guess, for he was given the nickname 'Cockney' by his shipmates. London was the greatest port in the world at that time so perhaps it was the sight of the great ships in the port, coming and going from all quarters of the world that inspired him.

"Perhaps if I had known what being a sailor really means I should not have been so anxious to go to sea. It is not all fun and frolic, as some people

seem to think; it is hard work and hard fare and hard study if you want to get on, and a lot of peril thrown in," he told Escott-Inman.

But that was what he wanted, so when he was fourteen he left school and his father obtained him an apprenticeship with the shipping firm of John Stewart & Co. of London and Charlie started his life at sea on the barque *Commonwealth*.

It was the beginning of a new century and a new era. After a reign of 64 years, Queen Victoria died in 1901, aged 82, and was succeeded by her eldest son Bertie who took the title Edward VII, his wife becoming Queen Alexandra. It was a very different world from today. Cars were a rarity, few homes had electricity or a telephone; women were demanding the right to vote (although in New Zealand they had been granted that right in 1893). In 1903 the first powered flights were made, in New Zealand by Richard Pearse and in United States of America by Orville and Wilbur Wright. Shipping was still the only means of transporting goods around the world at a time when manufacturing and trade were at their busiest.

Barques (or barks) were the work horses of the sea, carrying trade goods all over the world. A barque had three or more masts, with large square set sails, a type of rigging that was easier to manage than the rigging on the great schooners and clippers of the day, so they could be sailed with a smaller crew. The tallest mast was the mainmast, the second tallest, in front of the mainmast, was the foremast and the next in size, behind the mainmast, was the mizzenmast. As they hauled on the lines to raise or lower the sails one man would sing out the words of a sea shanty and the crew would join in the chorus, all pulling together to make the work easier.

Steam ships were becoming more generally used, but in 1900 there was still slightly more sail than steam on the high seas, especially the vessels that circumnavigated the world, mainly due to the problems of refueling the steam ships with coal or wood on a long voyage.

An apprenticeship lasted about seven years. It was the duty of an employer to train the apprentice in the skills of the job and to be responsible for his well-being. An apprentice would start as a deck boy or cabin boy before advancing to become an Ordinary Seaman. At the end, all being well, he would be qualified as an Able-Bodied Seaman and could then, if he wished and was capable, study for promotion to Second Mate, then First Mate and eventually he might even become a Captain, although that must have seemed a long way off to Charles Eyre when he started out.

For the next few years Charlie, still on the *Commonwealth*, travelled the world. It was a happy ship. "*- no boy would have wanted a better ship to start in, nor better captain and officers to sail under,*" he said later. This was important as the officers and crew were like a family, living closely together for weeks or months at a time. He enjoyed the life in spite of the long hours and hard work, experiencing hurricanes and storms, rounding the notoriously dangerous Cape Horn at the southern most tip of South America, more than once. Every night he spent some time reading books on seamanship, determined to make a success of his career.

Charlie was in Callao, when he learned that the *Commonwealth* had been sold. It was 1906 and he had not long completed his apprenticeship. His life was about to change.

It had been an eventful trip, right from the start. After seventeen days leave Charlie had received orders to join his ship at Rotterdam, in Holland. From there they sailed to Middlesbrough in the north of England where they picked up a cargo of pig-iron, iron bars two and a half feet long, each weighing roughly 200 pounds. They were bound for Australia, but they had no sooner set sail than they had to turn back to Falmouth in Cornwall for repairs because their cargo had broken loose and nearly smashed the sides out of the vessel. The damage was severe, the repairs delaying them for three months, but they made it to Australia eventually, unloading the pig-iron at Adelaide then sailing under ballast up the Australian coast to Newcastle where they took on a cargo of coal for Callao in Peru.

It was while they were at Newcastle that Charlie's apprenticeship expired, on 6 July 1906. He was now an AB or Able-Bodied Seaman, free to leave and join another ship if he wished, but he chose to sign on again with the same captain and sailed with the *Commonwealth* at the beginning of August.

The journey from New South Wales across the Pacific Ocean to Callao took them sixty-five days. When they got there they had to unload the coal themselves, that being the custom on the west coast of South America. In most ports the work would have been done by stevedores, shoremen employed for the task of loading and unloading cargo. " – *and working coal by hand is a dirty job – a thirsty, grimy, dusty job –*" Charlie described it. They had even had to clean the hold themselves.

And then came the news that the ship had been sold. It must have come as a considerable shock. She had been home to him ever since he had joined as an apprentice deck boy, fourteen years old and 'still wet behind the ears' as the First Mate told him. Now along with the rest of the crew he was out of a job. There must have been long and serious discussion among the crew about what to do next.

The two apprentice lads had already been found places aboard another ship belonging to the same company to continue their training. The rest of the men had two options. They could go home as passengers at the

Company's expense, or if they could find a berth on another ship they could sign on with her. The captain, the officers, the carpenter and the steward were the only ones to choose the first option. The others all decided to look for another ship.

Charlie did not explain why he preferred not to sail home as a passenger, but it may have been the thought of turning up on his mother's doorstep with hardly a penny to his name, for he would not get paid during the voyage. Better, surely, to work his passage home. In any case, a life of idleness was never attractive to him; he liked to be busy. Possibly it would be easier to find a ship in Callao than back in London. All he said was that he did not want to go home, so perhaps he just wanted more adventure.

Most of the men joined a barque called the *Ravenswood*, but Charlie and two other men, Walter Low and Harry Largerbloom (also given as Largilboni), had noticed another ship moored in the harbour. Charlie thought she looked fast, *'a real clipper'* he described her. She was a four-masted steel barque called the *Dundonald,* owned by Kerr and Newton of Glasgow.

He discussed it with the other men.

"That's a good ship," he said to Walter Low who nodded in agreement and Harry Lagerbloom added, *"I wouldn't mind sailing in her."*

The *Dundonald* was bound for Sydney where she would pick up a cargo of grain before returning to England, so Charlie approached his Captain and asked him if he would try to get him taken on as one of the crew. The captain agreed and shortly afterwards he told Charlie that the *Dundonald* was looking for three Able Seamen. Charlie was particularly pleased when the captain said, *"If you like to go, Eyre, I have arranged that you shall berth aft."*

That meant that Charlie would have a bunk in the stern, or rear of the ship, instead of the fo'c'sle, the forecastle at the front of the ship, where most of the crew had their quarters, which as Charlie put it – *"no matter how nice one's shipmates may be, a fo'c'sle is not the best place in the world to study in."* Now Charlie had completed his apprenticeship he was already looking to make it to Second Mate and was studying accordingly.

On 24 November Charlie, Walter and Harry went to the British Consul as they were legally bound to do, to be paid off the *Commonwealth* and signed on to the *Dundonald*. Harry was in fact a sailmaker, but the *Dundonald* already had a sailmaker so all three signed on as Able Bodied seamen. Both Walter and Harry were considerably older than twenty-one year old Charlie.

Early in December they set sail for Sydney. The *Ravenswood* had sailed ten days earlier along with another vessel called the *Annasona*, both bound for NSW.

There was no cargo on this trip, just ballast to keep her steady. Once again, Charlie was lucky in that the *Dundonald* was a happy ship. There were twenty-eight men and boys on board, including Captain Thorburne and his sixteen year old son, Jimmy. Jimmy had been ill and the doctors had recommended a sea voyage to improve his health. It must have seemed just the thing for him as they headed out across the Pacific.

The weather was fine and they made good time, fairly flying along some days with the wind billowing out the great square sails overhead and the sea-spray flying past the bows. They celebrated Christmas at sea and the new year, 1907, began.

Six days out from Sydney, though, the weather changed and a real southerly 'buster' blew up. The *Dundonald* rolled like a pig in mud, over on to her side one way, water breaking over her decks, then coming up with a lurch only to roll just as violently on to her other side. Things were certainly getting exciting, but Charlie had survived worse. He had just come off watch and was making himself comfortable below when the Captain himself appeared in the doorway.

"Eyre, my lad, will you get below and give a hand in the storeroom?" he asked.

He explained that the second mate was in the storeroom where many of the stores had broken loose and were in need of lashing up again. This easy almost fatherly way of giving orders seems to have been typical of Captain Thorburne and must have been one of the reasons for the happy running of the ship.

"Aye, aye, sir!" Charlie called promptly.

As he told the tale to Escott-Inman, Charlie found things even more lively down below. There was the Second Mate, Mr MacLaghlan, hot and sweating as he struggled to lash down boxes that had broken loose and bags that had torn open. Charlie had to leap clear as a barrel rolled towards his legs then he doubled over, half-winded, as a ham hurtled across the room and caught him in the midriff. Laughing at the chaotic scene, he dived in, cornering escaping tins, rounding up barrels, stowing them where they could do no more damage as the ship pitched and tossed.

When they finished at last they were plastered from head to foot with flour, oatmeal, marmalade, vinegar – but everything was safely secured and the storeroom was 'shipshape' once more. Charlie tells the tale as if it was all a huge joke, giving a sense of the cheerful, positive attitude he had to life in general which must have made him popular with his fellow crew mates. He seems to have got on particularly well with the Second Mate. On a Royal Navy ship there would have been a marked separation between officers and men with strict discipline insisted upon, but this was a civilian vessel, altogether more relaxed, although the Captain's word was still law.

The buster blew itself out at last and they arrived off Sydney Heads and picked up their tug to be towed into the harbour. They had made a record passage of forty-five days! The *Ravenswood* arrived a week later although they had sailed ten days before the *Dundonald*. I am sure Charlie and his two friends must have laughed at their old shipmates who had signed on with the slower vessel. They were justifiably proud of their new ship.

The ballast was unloaded and a cargo of wheat brought aboard, 36,000 bags of it. The ship moved out into the stream and dropped anchor, waiting for a tug to take them out to start their return voyage to Falmouth, England. It was a Saturday and the Australian sun was hot on their heads as they lined the deck watching a yacht race on the beautiful waters of Sydney Harbour. There was no tug available, but no one minded waiting until Monday.

The following day, Sunday 17 February, a tug was unexpectedly free to take them out and rather than lose another day Captain Thorburne gave the order to raise anchor. There was a stir of unease; no seaman likes to sail on a Friday and Sunday was considered just as unlucky.

It was only a superstition, but as if to prove their foreboding right the wind changed that very first night out and from then on they had head winds all the way.

With the wind coming straight at them from the very direction in which they wished to head there was nothing for it but to sail as near to the wind as they could, but every day their zig-zag course took them a little further from the direction they wished to go. After eight days everyone was watching the weather for a change, but when the change came it brought only a calm, hardly any wind at all, and what there was still blew head on to them.

The crew was bored, grumbling at the slow progress. Somehow not having enough to do can be just as tiring as battling the wind and waves, Charlie found, as yet another monotonous day dragged on.

Suddenly someone spotted a dark triangular fin cutting through the water. No one needed to be told what kind of fish it belonged to. The men clustered along the rail to see the shark glad of a bit of excitement. They marveled at the great size of the fish, wondering if they would be allowed to try and hook it.

The huge fish swam lazily along-side the ship as if curious about what kind of creature it was, possibly attracted by waste thrown overboard from the galley. Little blue pilot fish darted about its head, ready to feed on any scraps that escaped from the shark's mouth when it seized its next meal.

The men kept an eye on the poop deck where the Captain had his cabin. No one could throw out a line without the skipper's permission. Would he let them have a go at it? There was a buzz of excitement when Captain Thorburne strolled along for he had his big shark hook in his hand.

He called out to the 'doctor', meaning the cook, to bring a lump of salt pork from the galley. He baited the hook with the salt pork and threw it over the side. The shark veered off and circled around warily before making up its mind to take the bait, but at last it swam up to it, rolling onto its back so that its ugly wide mouth could grab the meat. The men groaned as it missed. It circled again, grabbed, missed. There were plenty of rude insults called out at the stupidity of the creature but at the fourth attempt, it swallowed the pork. Down its throat it went. The crew gave a cheer. The fight was on and what a battle it was.

The line was a good three inch rope, passed around the capstan to secure it while the men hauled the shark in, but they were afraid even that might not be strong enough hold such a large fish so they ran a bowline (similar to a kind of slipknot) down the rope so that it slipped over the shark's head. When the bowline was safely around the shark's body, they pulled the knot tight and heaved.

Up the side of the ship and on to the deck came the great fish, still thrashing and leaping and snapping while the men shouted warnings to each other.

Then a crew member, Sam Watson, finished it off with his knife and everyone had a bone to carve or a tooth to make into a necklace or a piece to cook – fresh fish made a pleasant change from salt meat.

Charlie tells, *"and as for me, I got hold of his tail; that was what I wanted. Perhaps you will smile when I tell you what I wanted it for. I have told you that we sailors are superstitious – well, one of our superstitions is that if you nail a shark's tail on to the end of the jib-boom you will have a fair wind for the rest of the journey."*

The jib-boom was the spar that the triangular sail at the bow of the ship was attached to. *"Alas, in our case, the superstition was not a true one,"* he added.

Indeed it was not as they were about to discover.

CHAPTER TWO

When the shark's tail was nailed to the jib, the superstitious sailors were hoping for a fair wind and in fact, after the calm, lazy day when they caught the shark, the weather did change, but not for the better. The wind roughened and they had nothing but rain, sleet, mist and heavy seas and still it was a head wind. To make matters worse, something was affecting the compass so that one minute the vessel would seem to be on course and the next minute the needle would have swung right round and the ship would appear to be going in the opposite direction. As Charlie put it, "*the steering compass went 'crook'.*"

In most places on earth, the compass needle does not point to the geographical north – in some places it points to the east of north, at others to the west of north. This is known as 'the variation of the compass' and an exact knowledge of the variation is of vital importance to a navigator. To make matters still more difficult, the magnetic pole does not remain constant; the direction changes. It was known that the magnetic south pole was moving northward, nearer to New Zealand, at that time.

The ship's compass would have been mounted on the binnacle in front of the ship's wheel. It would have had a large steel ball on each side of it, called Kelvin's Balls after Lord Kelvin who invented them in the 1880s. These could be adjusted to correct the magnetic field affecting the compass. It has been suggested that for the compass to go completely crazy as Charles Eyre described, it seems likely that one or both of the steel balls had come loose during the storm. As they moved to and fro with the pitch and roll of the ship the compass needle would have swung wildly. Another suggestion is that sun flares were affecting the weather and the magnetic field of the earth. Whatever the reason, it was to have disastrous consequences for the *Dundonald* and her crew.

With the rain pouring down from a heavily overcast sky there was no chance for the Captain to take a bearing with the sextant by measuring the angle between the sun and the horizon which would have enabled him to chart his position.

The days passed. Still there was no improvement. Wednesday 6 March came. Charlie took his turn at the wheel for a couple of hours then he was off duty until second dog watch – the two hours from six until eight o'clock in the evening. Now the weather began to turn really dirty. The main sail was already in and the fore and mizzen sails made fast. The order came for the main top-gallant sail to be secured. This meant going aloft, clambering up the rigging to tug and heave at the massive canvas sails, made even heavier by the rain which was falling in sheets. The wind howled around their ears, their fingers were raw and numb. It must have been a nightmare of a job and extremely dangerous.

Back on deck they struggled to coil loose ropes and lash down loose gear to keep it from being swept away by the great seas that constantly broke over the deck. To make matters worse a thick mist closed around the ship. Charlie could hardly see his hands in front of his face while the figures toiling around him loomed up out of the fog like ghosts.

All that could be done had been done; now they could only ride out the storm. Charlie was soaked through and chilled to the bone. With only half an hour to the end of his watch, he decided a mug of hot tea was needed. Mr MacLaghlan, the Second Mate, agreed. Charlie had his own little oil stove on which he sometimes brewed tea for himself and the Second Mate during the cold night watches. He lashed the stove so it could not shift and soon had a pan of water boiling on it. A handful of tea was thrown in. He felt it warming him as he drank it as hot as he could bear. He carried some out to the Second Mate.

It was to be the last tea any of them were to taste for months. As they stood side by side sipping it, *"growling at the weather"* as Charlie said, Mr MacLaghlan remarked, *"Don't show any signs of clearing."* He shielded the tin mug with his hands for the wind was strong enough to blow the tea right out of it. *"There is one comfort, it can't last for ever."*

The last quarter of an hour seemed unending with the shriek of the wind through the rigging, the *Dundonald* reeling from the force of the waves hammering into her. From the noise, the cold, the wet, Charlie said he was as tired as he had ever been in his life by the time their watch ended at last.

Down below, he stripped off his wet clothes. From his sea chest he grabbed the first dry vest that came to hand – it happened to be the oldest and thinnest he had - put it on and crawled into his bunk with a book. A young deck boy named George Ivimey was berthed with him. It was George's first voyage; he must have found it terrifying. Charlie himself could not have been too concerned about the storm for in spite of being bone tired he was determined to do his regular half hour of study before he went to sleep. He was working towards his second mate's examination.

After half an hour he put the book away and snuggled down to sleep, thinking he had a good three and a half hours before going on watch again. He was used to sleeping in short snatches, regardless of noise and movement around him, but he had hardly closed his eyes when a cry pierced the roar of the storm.

"All hands on deck!"

Charlie assumed they needed help with the sails. Neither he nor George Ivemey fancied getting out of their warm bunks and for a moment neither of them moved, but then they heard, *"Land on the weather bow, sir!"*

Land! It was an ominous call. Any sailor would know that land where no land was expected spelled danger. Charlie was out of his bunk in an instant. He pulled on a pair of dungaree trousers – poor, thin things as it happened - and a pair of hefty sea-boots. He grabbed a coat, an oilskin and a sou'wester (a waterproof hat with a brim especially wide at the back that kept the rain from running down his neck) and, last of all, his knife. Still clutching the clothes, he rushed up on to deck. What he saw sent him tearing back to warn George Ivimey.

Charlie tells how he yelled at George.

*"Hurry, man! Hurry! Get your gear on!"*as he struggled into his outer garments before racing back on deck.

Forging ahead through the storm and the fog, the *Dundonald* had come up without warning on a black, forbidding headland. She was being driven headlong into a narrow bay with sides of sheer, volcanic rock, the tops lost in the mist. Great rolling waves crashed against the cliffs – Charlie described them as *"great, unbroken monsters"*, sending huge columns of spray high into the air. Writhing like black snakes in the foam were masses of seaweed, strands twenty feet long and as thick as a man's wrist.

It must have been obvious to every man that they were doomed. The ship seemed bound to smash headlong into the cliffs and no vessel would survive that. There was just one slim chance; Captain Thorburne knew it and calmly he gave the orders to wear the ship round. The crew sprang into action, hauling and straining with all their might on the yard arms to swing the ship round, away from that rocky face. Round she came, but oh, so slowly, and all the time she was being driven by the waves closer to the shore. It was going to be a near thing – *if* she made it.

Suddenly the *Dundonald* gave a mighty shudder, like a living thing, as she struck a submerged reef. The next minute she had been carried over it by the sheer force of the waves. The vessel had to have been damaged by such a blow, but there was no time to stop and think about that: they had been ordered to swing the yards and swing them they would until they were told to stop, even though they knew it was hopeless – there just wasn't room to bring her round.

Walter Low, his old mate from the *Commonwealth*, was working alongside Charlie who, having no idea of where they were, yelled to him.

"Where are we, anyhow?"

"Stewart Island," Walter called back, believing they were off the south coast of New Zealand. He could not have been more mistaken. They were far south of New Zealand, 50° 40′ south in fact, in sub-Antarctic waters.

Somehow they succeeded in turning the ship right around. She was still closing in on the land, but stern first now and only slowly. Some of the men must have clung to a glimmer of hope for the carpenter asked Charlie if he thought they could 'weather' the land, that is, avoid it. Charlie told him no.

The cry came from the Mate to release the topsail halyard; the ropes that hauled and lowered the sails. They rushed to obey and down came the three heavy yards when another order came.

"Clear the boats, lads!"

They all knew what that meant: the ship could not be saved and they must leave her while they could, although in fact it must have been plain that there was little hope of lowering the boats in those conditions.

The two lifeboats were on wooden skids, which formed a kind of bridge about twenty feet wide from one side of the deck to the other. Charlie, his hands almost numb with the cold, cut away at the canvas cover over the nearest boat. Suddenly, amid all the noise, the howling, the unearthly moaning, the crashing and the creaking, he became aware that he could hear no voices. He looked up. He was alone. For one terrible moment he wondered if a monster wave had swept his mates all away – he knew they would never have deserted him willingly. Then, through the mist, he glimpsed a shadowy figure making its way aft and other forms moving, too.

There was nothing he could do single-handed where he was, so he struggled after them and found the Captain and the whole ship's company gathered on the poop where normally only officers and men on duty were allowed. The helmsman was still sticking gamely to his post at the wheel. As Charlie told Escott-Inman, *"You may talk of this hero and that, but to my mind, I looked at a hero then. He was only a common seaman, a Swede named Andersen, but standing there at the wheel, as though he were out in mid-ocean, with no peril nigh."*

Charlie described the sounds; they must have been eerily scary. *"The air was full of strange noises now – wind voices, and sea voices, moaning, sobbing voices, as of storm spirits, singing the dirge of the fated ship."*

The fact that in all the frantic, near hopeless struggle there was no panic is a tribute to the good discipline on board and the trust the men had in their captain and the officers. It had been a happy, well-run ship and now this paid off. Orders were carried out promptly without question, the men working together in spite of their fear, for every one of them must have been deadly afraid.

The Captain ordered the men to put on life-belts. These were stored in a locker below. The ship's sail-maker braved the seas breaking over the deck to fetch them and they were handed out by the Second Mate, one to every man. His teeth chattering with cold, Charlie fumbled with the strings that fastened his belt around him.

In spite of all the chaos around him, Andersen was still at the wheel. He asked the Captain if he should leave it when the ship struck, as it was bound to do.

"Leave it now, man," the Captain said. *"You can do no more good there now."*

Andersen had hardly released his grip on the spokes of the wheel when a tremendous wave caught the rudder and sent the wheel spinning. The next instant the rudder struck a rock. The sudden stopping of it broke the wheel into pieces. If there had been any chance at all before, it was gone now. The ship was drifting out of control, nearer and nearer to the cliffs.

As he waited for the end Charlie noticed a great tunnel-like cave in the cliff. The waves rushed through it and out the other side with a weird, hollow sound so dismal that it chilled his heart.

In the blackness of the night, with the icy blast of the wind, the slanting rain and the mist, all was confusion, but Charlie could feel that the deck was tilting under his feet. The ship had run aground on a shelf of sunken rock and was no longer drifting towards land, but was slowly keeling over on to her side. They could tell from the waves that there was still deep water between the ship and the shore. Now they could only wait.

They clustered together. For days now the Captain had seen no sun from which to calculate their position. Relying on dead reckoning, worked out from time and speed, he had expected to pass the Auckland Islands some forty miles to windward but now it was clear to him that these were the islands they had struck. These islands are 465km (290 miles) south of New Zealand and under New Zealand protection. At least there would be

Government supply depots on shore, Captain Thorburne assured the men, established especially for ship-wrecked sailors like themselves.

I think Charlie was a realist who knew pretty well what the situation was. In his account he says that the crew did not quite know what to make of their position, but that he believed the Captain knew.

"I looked into his face several times – it was as calm and unmoved as ever – and yet there was something there which I had not seen before."

Jabez Peters, the First Mate, suggested moving forward where they might find a little more shelter. Clinging to whatever they could grasp, they slipped and slithered their way to the bow of the ship. Already the sea was making breaches in the sides. They could feel the ship shiver under the weight of the blows and they were at constant risk from wreckage that was washing across the deck. They huddled under the overhang of the fo'c'sle. Every man there knew all too well the danger they were in, but still there was no panic.

The Captain could not have been the only one to understand their danger, but Mr Peters in particular seems to have shown great calmness and courage which must have been a comfort to the men. He took out his pipe, knocked the ashes out of it and carefully filled the bowl with tobacco from his pouch for one last smoke.

"We shan't be able to stay here long," he remarked. He patted his pockets, looking for a match. *"Any of you fellows got a match?"* he asked.

Jack Puhze produced a new box.

"Here you are, sir. They're quite dry."

The First Mate took them with a nod and thanked the man. He struck a match, shielding it with his hand, bending over the tiny red flame that glowed on his face. He handed the box back to Jack.

"Thanks," he said again and drew on his pipe.

Jack Puhze looked at the box of matches. Thinking they were of no use to him now, he raised his arm to toss them into the sea.

At the last second something inspired Charlie to grab his hand. He said, *"Hold on, Jack. Give them to me. They may come in handy."*

Jack looked surprised; I imagine he wondered what use Charlie would have for matches fathoms deep in the ocean, but he gave them to Charlie who unbuttoned his oilskin and tucked the box away in an inside pocket. I wonder, did Charlie, in spite of everything, still cling to a glimmer of hope that they might survive?

Another big sea broke over them. The Captain said they would have to move as it had become clear they would be trapped there, drowned without a chance, if they didn't soon get to a higher point. They had hardly made it up on to the fo'c'sle head when waves began to crash one after the other across the main deck. Below was wild sea; above them now only rigging.

Captain Thorburne glanced down at his young son. His face was sad. Charlie heard him mutter to Mr Peters, *"Take care of him, Mister."*

The next moment a truly monstrous wave rose clear over the forecastle head. It seemed to hang over their heads then down it crashed upon them.

Charlie clung on like grim death as the wave dragged him away. Then it was gone. The ship seemed to be falling down, down, into a deep hollow, walls of water rising higher and higher above it until down they came and filled in the watery grave. The *Dundonald* was buried.

CHAPTER THREE

With the sea crashing down upon him, Charlie clung desperately to the ship's rail, but the water tore him away, as helpless as a leaf, whirled him round, pressed him down and down for what felt like forever. Sparkling lights danced before his eyes, caused by oxygen starvation as his lungs fought for breath. Then he was thrown up against what he later realised must have been a tangle of rigging for his fingers closed around a rope and with the last of his strength he began to haul himself upwards until he could gasp in a lungful of blessed air. At first he was too exhausted to move, but his cork life-belt buoyed him up and he hung on, gasping, while he tried to gather his wits.

The ship was lying on her side, her masts leaning towards the land. The top gallant yard arm appeared to be actually touching the cliff. Charlie judged that if he could just climb higher, then work his way along the yard, he could scramble to safety.

Weighed down by his wet clothes and heavy boots, he painfully inched his way up the rigging, out along the yard arm towards land only to face bitter disappointment. His eyes had deceived him. Between the end of the yard arm and the streaming cliff there was a gap of a good twenty feet.

Close to despair, he heard a voice say, *"Is that you, Charlie?"*

Charlie turned sharply. Another man, the Irishman John Judge, was close up behind him. I can imagine his relief to find that there was another soul alive besides himself.

John Judge clearly had the same fear for, shouting above the noise of the storm, he said, *"Charlie, I think we two are the only ones left of us all and God knows how long we'll last or if we'll ever get ashore. We'll never leap that."*

Charlie could only agree. Judge, however, was a man who thought carefully about things and he suggested that there might be a way to swing across the gap.

He explained his idea. If they cut some lines from the rigging and made one end fast to the yard arm, they could put a bowline on the other end and try to swing across. A bowline is a slip knot with a double loop. Judge thought it possible to sit in the loop and swing across the gulf. It was a slim chance at best, but they were desperate. If only he had a knife!

Charlie, however, did have one. He pulled out his sheath knife and passed it to John who set to and cut a good length of rope from the tangle of rigging all around them. Charlie fastened it firmly to the yard arm, but it was still too short. They needed more, so John hacked away again, but then Charlie heard him give a horrified cry of dismay.

"What? What's the matter?"

"I've dropped the knife, Charlie. We are done for entirely now!"

It was another crushing disappointment. All they could do now was huddle together for warmth, perched above the seething water, praying that the mast would stay firm while they waited for the new day to dawn. As they listened to the wind, to the crash and boom of the waves, they thought they could hear cries of distress and once an awful shriek. His wet clothes were heavy. His sea-boots were like lead weights on his feet. He kicked them off and let them drop—an action he came to regret.

The rain never ceased, but at last the first streaks of grey in the sky told them it was morning. As the gloomy light increased they were able to look around. It must have been a grim sight, but suddenly Charlie saw another figure clinging on to the rigging below them. He pointed him out to John Judge.

They were almost too stiff and cold to move, but they made their way slowly down to where they found not one but nine of their shipmates perched like wet crows on the mast and rigging. Every one of them was gashed or battered from the wreckage or even by the rocks for some of them told how they had been swept clean off the ship and back on to it again. Both the First Mate, Mr Peters, and the Second Mate, Mr MacLaghlan, were there, although Mr Peters was in a bad way from the battering he had received. There was no sign of the Captain or his young son.

There seemed little hope for any of them. The island was so near, but such a fierce sea raged between them that it might as well have been fifty miles away. Anyone venturing into the water would have been smashed to pulp within minutes. All the same, Charlie felt better for seeing the other men. In his own words, *"for though it did not lessen our peril, there was something of comfort feeling that one's companions were there. It took away that awful feeling of loneliness which I had at first experienced."*

After a while Mr Peters suggested that one thing they could do was to cut a few lines of rope. He said it might come in handy if any of them reached the shore.

There did not appear to be much chance of that, but Charlie thought it would give him something to do and the exercise might get a bit of warmth into his frozen limbs.

Mr Peters was too weak to do much himself, but he lent his big clasp knife to Charlie who opened it and, holding the knife between his teeth, began to climb higher up the rigging. He cut away several long lines, coiling them around his body. But he needed more. He started to climb higher still, but suddenly he stopped, hardly able to believe his eyes.

As he told Escott-Inman, *"There, through the grey, misty light, I saw a face looking across at me from the cliff. Was I wandering-- was it a ghost – or what? No. it was a real face, it belonged to one of our crew. There, on the cliff was one of our ordinary seamen – Michael Pul by name."*

With real hope at last, Charlie yelled the news to the men below. It was a huge relief to them all. Not only was he glad to see Michael had survived, but all along they had been aware that their biggest problem would be how to get a line from the ship to the shore with no way of attaching it to anything, but now there was someone there to secure it! Charlie slashed and hacked at the strongest rope he could find, aware that it was to be the life-line for them all.

First he made one end fast to the upper top-gallant yardarm. Then he threw the other end with all his might. Michael Pul had been watching and was ready to catch it. As soon as he had it in his hand he tied it firmly around a large craggy rock. They had a bridge.

It looked to be about fifteen feet long and it would be a risky business swinging hand over hand across it to where Michael Pul waited, but now two more figures appeared out of the mist. Amazingly their numbers were increasing. First there had just been Charlie and John Judge, then another nine, then Michael and now two more, making fourteen survivors. Then a faint cry from below reached their ears. Perched on a narrow ledge of rock was yet another pair. They were clinging on just above the waves, drenched with spray at every moment, unable to climb either up or down. The other men shouted down words of encouragement, but before anyone could help them they had to get across that thin rope bridge.

The men were half-frozen, cut and bleeding, exhausted by their struggles throughout the night and so weak they could hardly crawl let alone haul themselves across above those fearsome rocks. As Charlie told Escott-Inman, *"the hope of safety acted like a spur"* and one by one they all made it across. They had to make a bowline for Mr Peters to sit in and be pulled across for he was too badly injured to get over by himself.

When all the men were safely across, a line was lowered to the pair stranded on the ledge — only to find that it was too short. With stiff, cold fingers they had to separate the strands of the rope into two parts and knot the two lengths together. The rope was thinner and not so strong, but it held and the last two men were finally brought to the top.

If the *Dundonald* had not been a sailing ship with plenty of rope rigging it is hard to imagine any of them would have made it to land — and of course all the crew knew their knots. Their resourcefulness and courage was to be fully tested in the weeks to come.

Sixteen men gathered, shivering and bleeding, in the grey morning light. It was a sad moment as they counted those who had survived — and those who were missing. Besides Charles Eyre himself and John Judge, those who had made it so far were the Mates Jabez Peters and Daniel MacLaghlan, the third officer Karl Knudsen from Norway, Santiago Marino from Chile, Alf Findlow, George Ivimey, Jack Puhze, Jack Stewart and the cabin boy Albert Roberts who was only fourteen years old. The three on the cliff top were Michael Pul from Estonia, Harry Walters from Norway and Herman Querfeldt from Germany. The last two men, rescued from the ledge, were the Australian Bob Ellis and the Irishman Mickey Grattan.

There seemed little hope that they would find anyone else, but their spirits rose when someone reminded them of the Captain's words, that if these were truly the Auckland Islands then there would be a Government depot not too far away with food, blankets and clothing.

Over the years there had been many wrecks on these islands. Sealers had reported wreckage on the islands as early as the 1830s. In the days before radio made communication possible between ship and shore, it was not unusual for a vessel to be lost at sea, never to be heard of again. One such ship was the *Dunedin*, the first ship to successfully carry a cargo of refrigerated meat from New Zealand to Britain in 1882. She vanished at sea in 1890. In January 1864, the *Grafton* had been driven on to the rocks in Carnley Harbour during a storm. All five men reached shore. In May that same year, the *Invercauld* had been wrecked off the north west of the main island. Nineteen made it to land, but only three survived; the others died from starvation. It seems incredible that the two groups were on the island at the same time but neither saw a trace of the other – until you consider the kind of rough, mountainous land they found themselves in.

After that supplies began to be left at various points for shipwrecked mariners. In May 1866 the *General Grant* was wrecked on the west coast. Fifteen made it ashore; ten survived, but did not find the supplies. It was the following year that the government ordered three provision huts to be built on Auckland Island for castaways, but it was not until January 1868 that the ten survivors were rescued. Another depot was built on Enderby Island. Each depot was to be checked for survivors twice a year.

This must have been in Jabez Peters' mind as he tried to encourage the crew of the *Dundonald*. They must head north-east, he advised, knowing there was a depot there and another in the south of the island.

They set off immediately for by now they were all desperately hungry. It was tough going, up a steeply sloping hillside covered with coarse, scrubby grass and low, tangled bushes. There were no trees and no sign of fresh water, but nesting on the ground was a vast number of mollymawks, the New Zealand white-capped albatross, a large bird with a wingspan of between 180cm and 250cm. They showed no fear, watching the men curiously, not attempting to fly away as they had never encountered men before.

At least they would be able to catch and eat the birds, Charlie thought, if the worst came to the worst. He did not fancy the idea, though, and struggled on, intent on finding the depot.

They were still only halfway up the side of the mountain when, swift and silent, a thick blanket of mist came rolling down. It closed around them, blotting out everything so that they hardly dared take a step for fear of falling over a precipice or into a crevasse. There was nothing for it but to stop and wait for it to clear. They huddled together, faint with hunger, perished with the cold. Their misery seemed complete when the icy, penetrating rain began to fall again.

By mid-afternoon they were all so hungry that they were ready to eat anything - even raw mollymawk. It was easy enough to catch and skin the birds, but there was no way of cooking them. They gritted their teeth and chewed the raw meat, glad of any food at all.

Still the rain fell and while they waited for the mist to lift they exchanged survival stories. Mickey Grattan and Bob Ellis had crawled along the upper top-sail yard to the ledge, only to discover that they were no better off until they were found.

Michael Pul, Harry Walters and Herman Querfeldt were able to tell Charlie what had become of his old friend Walter Low. Walter had led the other three to the after-mast at the stern which he had discovered was actually hard up against the cliff face, although some way below the top. Walter was determined to scale the cliff although there was hardly enough finger or toe hold for a mouse. The others followed his example: they made it, but Walter slipped and was not seen again. Nor were many others. They heard how the steward had shut himself in the cabin moments before a massive explosion as the air pressure blew the skylight out. The charthouse was washed away, and every lifeboat smashed and washed overboard.

Naturally enough, the men wondered where exactly they were. Where was Auckland Island?

Mr Peters told them that it was actually a group of islands. Auckland Island was the largest, but there was Adams Island to the south and Enderby and several smaller ones to the north and to the west. He said they were about two hundred and seventy miles south of New Zealand and that Auckland Island had actually been settled for a time; a venture that lasted less than three years before the people gave up and were taken off.

He was referring to a settlement started in 1849. A fishing company, owned by Charles Enderby had been given government backing to set up a whale fishery at Port Ross in the north of the main island. They called the settlement Hardwicke. As well as a fishery, it was intended to be a farming settlement and a place where ships could be supplied and repaired. A community of about 150 European settlers tried to farm, but found the conditions too harsh and gave up in 1852. A number of Maori had settled on Auckland Island in 1841 and they lasted longer, but finally gave up in 1854.

Slowly the day passed, and then the night. Without his sea-boots, Charlie's feet were so cold that he dug a little hole in the ground, put them into it and covered them with earth. That helped a little. Santiago Marino went off to catch more sea birds. They tasted awful, but the still-warm food helped keep their strength up.

Morning came at last. The mist lifted and they were able to struggle on, the thought of food and fire at the end of the journey keeping them going. Charlie was not the only man without boots. Many of them had shed their heavy sea boots and outer gear for fear it would weigh them down in the water. Now, in places, their feet left smears of blood on the rocky patches of ground. At other times they sank ankle-deep into swampy mud between tussocks of rough grass, but they made it to the summit at last and looked out at the scene ahead and below.

They saw rocks and scrub and grass, mollymawks dotted everywhere like fat white daisies, and they saw the sea — sea all around them. They were on a small, bleak, desolate little island some three miles long and two miles wide — and there were still eight kilometres (six miles) of raging sea between them and the main Auckland Island!

CHAPTER FOUR

For several minutes no one could speak; they were beyond words. In Charles Eyre's words, *"We were on a bleak, barren island about three miles long and two wide. No trace of water, no sign of life of any sort could we see! All silence, all mountain, and scrub and loneliness, and all around the waves... We did not know the name of the island then, yet in our minds we named it aright – it was indeed Disappointment Island."*

They had struck its west coast. It was well named; this tiny island to the west of the main island was the only one that had no supply depot.

Their most pressing need was fresh water to drink. They split up into five groups to search for it, arranging to meet back at an agreed point to report on their findings. Wearily Charlie dragged himself up the slope. It was hard going over rough tussock grass. There were a few low scrubby bushes, but no trees. Suddenly he heard a shout. Someone had found a pool. They hurried towards the spot, threw themselves flat on the ground and scooped up the water in their hands.

The first taste had Charlie spluttering. The water was not as salty as the sea, but it was too briny to be any good for drinking. By now they were so thirsty that they drank the stuff anyway, but all too soon a raging thirst gripped them and stomach cramps had them doubled over in pain. Remembering the bitter taste, Charlie even wondered if minerals from the volcanic rock had poisoned the water.

They were soaked to the skin and their mouths were moist with rain, but what they needed was water to swallow. As the little groups straggled back to the meeting place, they all reported the same: there was no fresh water to be found.

Mr Peters insisted. There must be water somewhere. He reasoned that all the rain must collect somewhere. They must keep looking till they found it.

As he encouraged them sunshine broke through the clouds, the first they had seen for days. The effect was amazing. They immediately felt more hopeful and when Mr Peters suggested they return to the wreck and see if they could salvage anything from it the men agreed. As the Mate said, it was better than sitting there idle.

It is notable that even in their present dire situation, the men still referred to the ship's officers as Mister, showing a respect that must have been earned by their past leadership. A weak or unpopular officer would soon have lost all authority in the circumstances. Both Jabez Peters and Second Mate Daniel MacLaghlan were strong leaders, well respected, and this went a long way to keep the men from giving up in despair when all hope seemed lost. Even though he was desperately ill, Mr Peters kept encouraging the men to do what they could to survive.

A few men were too weak to go any further, but most of the crew began to make their way back down the long slope they had climbed so painfully. It was too hard; before they were halfway there they collapsed to the ground, faint from hunger and weak from the ill-effects of the bad water they had swallowed. The sun went in again and a chill, damp wind bit into their bones. They could see the wreck of the *Dundonald* below. The sea was breaking her up. Already some of the masts were gone. In time nothing would remain.

What they needed more than anything was warmth. Unless they could find a way to start a fire they would perish. Mr Peters muttered what he would give for a box of matches.

Until that moment Charlie had forgotten the matches he had tucked away previously. Now he called out that he had some.

"Don't you remember? I took the box from Jack Puhze."

Everyone gathered around him eagerly as he fished the box out of his pocket. Not surprisingly, the box was soaked with sea water and most of the matches useless, but at the bottom were a few that did not seem so very wet. They might light. Charlie was afraid he would drop them, his hands were shaking so much.

Harry Walters took the box from him saying he would try. He had noticed some withered sort of stuff just down the slope that might burn.

Other men searched their pockets and two more boxes were found, but they still had only twelve good matches among them.

They watched, hardly daring to hope, as Harry with two or three other men climbed down to a patch of the bramble-like bushes in the lee of the hill, out of the worst of the weather. It seemed like ages, but at last a thin wisp of smoke was seen rising. It grew thicker until there was a regular column spiralling upwards. A cheer went up and the men staggered down to gather round it.

Then they hurried to gather more wood, armfuls of anything that would burn. They had a fire and they would make good and sure not to let it go out again. They managed to gather together enough to keep the flames fed.

It was Mr MacLaghlan who reminded them that time was passing and they still had not gone down to the wreck. Some of the men could not see what use the ship was to them now. There was nothing but 'sticks' above water. The 'sticks' were her masts.

Mr MacLaghlan brushed away their doubts, saying that those 'sticks' had ropes and spars and good sails on them and that a sail made a good tent which was a great deal better than lying out in the open.

They built up a good big fire that would burn for a long time then those men who were strong enough made their way down to the wreck. The *Dundonald* had slipped even further on to her side so that now the highest yard arm was actually touching the cliff so, although it was not exactly easy, it was possible to reach it and start detaching the first sail. It was a risky business with the ship breaking up under the hammering of the waves. Even as they worked they could feel the masts tremble as if they might go at any moment.

They managed to free two sails which they hauled up to where the fire still burned; hissing as the rain drops fell into it.

"Now lads, pull up some sods of earth and build a wall," urged Mr MacLaghlan, so they tore up great clumps of the coarse grass, roots and all, and piled them into a low wall. Then they stretched the canvas sail between the wall and the ground, with more clods pinning it down so that the wind could not blow it away.

As the fire blazed fiercely, fanned by the savage wind, they huddled beneath the canvas sail. They had shelter and warmth, now all they needed was dinner.

"Now then, who's coming bird catching?" someone asked. Following Daniel MacLaghlan's example they made an effort to sound brave and cheerful. It must have taken great resolve to venture out into the bitter wind again, but they had to eat. Charlie set off with a group of other men.

The mollymawks sat on their high round nests. They opened their hooked beaks, clattering them indignantly and hissing at the strangers, but the men were hungry. They returned to camp with enough to feed everyone.

Those who had not taken part in catching dinner turned to and cooked it. The birds were skinned, skewered on pointed sticks and laid on the hot embers for half an hour. They were rather burnt on the outside and somewhat under-done on the inside but they were vastly better than raw meat.

Only Mr Peters was too ill to eat. Uncomplaining, he encouraged every effort they made, never letting them give in to despair, but he was growing weaker all the time. He was an older man than most of the crew and it is probable that he had suffered internal injuries.

Before settling down for the night the men built up a good supply of wood for the fire. They worked out shifts so that two men were always on watch to keep it in and not just for warmth; if a ship passed in the night and saw the blaze they would be rescued. Already they were showing the teamwork and cooperation that could possibly save them.

The last watch of the night was shared by Charlie and the Australian, Bob Ellis. It was a strange time. Charlie described "the sense of silence and noise" as one of the most weird experiences of his life as he and Bob sat at the entrance to their makeshift tent and kept watch.

"The wind moaned and sobbed, and then screamed again all around until it seemed like the cries of some demon in torment and mingling with the wind came the deeper roar of the sea as it fretted and beat at the foot of the cliff."

"Then, again and again, rising above these deeper sounds, there would come the shrill screams of the night birds and seagulls – strange eerie sounds that made one start and shiver as they listened. And yet with it all there was that oppressive sense of solitude."

He was very aware of how far they were from the regular shipping routes, almost as far south as the Antarctic Circle. He must have been feeling understandably downcast when he asked Bob if he thought they would ever get away from that place.

Bob shook his head. He could not say. He did know they needed to get to the main island. After a while Charlie remarked that the mate seemed bad and Bob agreed. Mr Peters had not been able to eat and the water was poison to him. It was poison to all of them Charlie must have thought. They must find fresh water soon or they would all be done for.

As dawn broke, cold and grey, Charlie made his way to where the birds were nesting. He returned with half a dozen which Bob cooked for their breakfast. Bob had noticed the seaweed lower down the slope. He had heard of fellows eating seaweed, he said, and suggested they gave it a try. It might give the birds a bit of flavor.

Charlie agreed. He set off and gathered an armful of the mossy green stuff. Now they had vegetables with the poultry, he joked. The seaweed had a salty, medicinal taste, but it was not too unpleasant. When you're hungry enough almost anything tastes all right, he recalled thinking.

The other men were awake now, preparing their breakfasts. Lack of water was still their greatest worry. A heated discussion soon broke out.

Harry Walters said that it seemed to him that since there was no water on this island they would have to leave.

"Leave? Tell us how, man, and we'll leave fast enough!"

Harry said they should make a raft. They objected, rightly enough, that you needed timber to build a raft, but there was not a tree to be found. They clearly could not use the bramble-like stuff they were burning.

Harry, jerked his thumb towards the wreck. There was timber there, good stout spars, and they were sitting there letting the sea take them away when they could be the saving of the men.

Charlie demanded to know how they were going to get them. Even if they got two or three of the spars he could not see how they would get them ashore. There was no beach and a mighty big sea running.

Harry was unwilling to give up the idea. He still felt it could be done.

Mr MacLaghlan shook his head. He agreed with Charlie. He said the water must be at least sixty fathoms deep around the wreck. They would never get them ashore.

Harry was not about to give up. He insisted they could at least try. He said that around the point they could get right down to the water's edge. If they could free any of the spars they could tow them around and haul them up on to the beach. It was only six miles to the other island and they could manage that on a raft.

Charlie still thought it was madness and most of the men agreed with him. Even if they got the spars and made a raft – how would they steer it? There was a powerful current between the two islands. They would be carried away south before they got halfway across.

Harry retorted that they would die if they stayed where they were and if there was any chance he was for taking it and Bob Ellis added that for sure they could not be any worse off than they were. Still most of the men were unconvinced, perhaps unsurprisingly after the ordeal of the wreck. They were on solid ground where they were, they had food of a kind and they would find water if they kept looking.

Harry scowled. He muttered that he could not do it by himself. If no-one would help him he would have to forget the whole idea, although it was a crying shame to see those spars drifting out to sea and not make an effort to get any of them.

Charlie looked down at the wreck. Harry was right about that. He still thought the raft idea was crazy, but if they could get one of the spars they might be glad of it. Perhaps they were persuaded by Harry's persistence for Mr MacLaghlan said, *"Well, it'll give us something to do. If Walters thinks there's a chance, let's take it."*

This argument shows clearly how each man felt free to express his opinion and how disagreements were resolved without hard feelings. There was a willingness to try anything that might improve their chances of surviving.

As the *Dundonald* had been a steel ship, there was a limited amount of timber available for salvage, but after a great deal more discussion it was decided that it might be possible to get the fore-upper-top-gallant yard. The yards were the cross spars that the sails hung from. They set to work – and heavy work it was, cutting away rigging, unshackling gear, fastening a rope from one end of the yard to a rock on land. It was growing dark when they gave up for the day and returned to build up the wood pile for the night and make a meal of mollymawks and seaweed, but the next morning they returned and soon the yard was freed and ready to be dropped into the sea.

Down it came with a most tremendous splash and then the men saw just how fierce the current was for it took all their combined strength to hold it from being dragged away. Grimly they hung on to the line they had attached to it and began to haul it around the point to a spot where they hoped to beach it. Halfway there the line snapped. Two days hard labour was swept away. The sea had won again.

That night Charlie turned in and tried to make himself as comfortable as he could under the sailcloth which was all the roof they had. It was a dark night, the moon hidden by a thick layer of cloud. It was hard to sleep, though, with the wind howling and the sea thundering. He did not think he would ever get used to it. Suddenly a new noise – an eerie shrieking, whistling sound – made him sit bolt upright, the hairs on his neck and arms bristling. All round him the other men were waking, wondering what the strange noise could be. Someone said it sounded like birds.

"What? Birds at this time of night?"

"May be owls."

"Maybe donkeys! Owls hoot; and besides the place would want to be crowded with owls for them to make that row."

There was only one way to find out. They groped their way outside. In the blackness around them they could see nothing, but still the unearthly whistling went on around them. Suddenly one of the men cried out as he went tumbling over.

Indignantly he demanded to know who had hit him. They assured him that none of them had done it, but someone or something had knocked him over. Then another man cried out that something had hit him in the eye and nearly knocked it out. A third man was struck. The air was full of shrieks and a strange whirring sound and cries of alarm as more men were hit. They beat a hasty retreat to the tent where they debated whether it was birds – or ghosts!

The next night was cloudless and moonlit and they slept undisturbed, but the following night was overcast again and once more the air was full of shrieks and whistles and small whirring bodies. The only way to solve the mystery was to catch one and the next time a man was hit he grabbed the feathery missile and hung on to it.

In the morning they examined it. It was a seabird about the size of a pigeon. They had seen no other birds apart from the mollymawks in that place, although later they saw many on the island, but knew the names of none of them. These they simply called 'night birds'. In fact they were mutton birds that instead of nesting like the mollymawks, lived in burrows.

Mutton birds are sooty shearwaters, a favourite food of some Maori people who dig out the fat young chicks in the burrows, skin them, dry them and store them for later. Today you can buy them, at a price, in some food markets.

The shearwaters explained the numerous holes they had noticed, honeycombing the ground. More than once a man had gone through the surface to find himself knee deep in a burrow. During the day and on bright nights the birds remained hidden but on moonless or cloudy nights they came out in their hundreds to feed at sea, then returned to land, flying in hard and fast at just the height to catch a man full in the face. They were a real danger and few men ventured out on cloudy nights for fear of getting an eye knocked out.

They were too small and too hard to find in their burrows to be worth hunting for food when there were mollymawks to be had so they were mostly left alone at that time.

CHAPTER FIVE

The need for water was becoming desperate. Again and again the conversation came back to the problem. So far they had existed on rain from the sky and the bitter salty stuff that collected in hollows among the rocks. Charlie Eyre and Bob Ellis talked together.

Bob insisted that it was no use staying where they were. They had to have water and there was none there. They would have to look for a better spot.

When Charlie said he did not think the others would move, Bob said that in that case he would go alone. He said they did not even know what was on the other side of the mountain. They had only seen it from the top.

Mr Peters would not be able to go, Charlie warned him. The First Mate was growing weaker every day. Bob still insisted that at least some of them could go. He was determined to go himself. Charlie could see that what Bob said made sense and after hesitating a while said he would go with him.

They told the others what they planned to do. Mr Peters, as Charlie had said, was too ill to go and Mr MacLaghlan and the Third Officer, Karl Knudsen, would not leave him.

Mr MacLaghlan gave them his approval, telling them to take one of the sails for shelter and if they found anything let them know.

Some of the men had lost heart and had neither the will nor the strength to make the effort, but four or five others said they couldn't be any worse off and they might as well give it a go. Early the next morning they set off. They took four of the precious matches with them and one of the sails, each man taking his turn to carry it in a long roll on his shoulder.

It must have been a heavy, clumsy burden and Charlie admitted they were often tempted to dump it as they as they toiled, one behind the other, up the hillside, or waded through mud and over tussock in the wind and rain, through flurries of hail or sleet which half blinded them. Again and again they had to stop to catch their breath but they were determined to press on. When they stopped at last, late in the afternoon, as Charlie described

"- we were all properly done and could not crawl another yard, so we were compelled to stay where we were and make our camp for the night. All through that day we had neither food nor drink; and we had been reduced to such a state that we had actually plucked at the grass and weeds, and had striven to eat them, in the hopes that they would stay the horrible torments of hunger and thirst..."

They used one of the matches to light a fire, although there was little wood around to keep it burning. Charlie was on his way to catch mollymawks for a meal when a shriek split the air. It made the hair on his neck stand up for a moment – until he made out the words.

"Water! Water! Fresh water!"

It was only a small pool with dead grass and slime floating on it, but Charlie said he had never tasted anything so delicious as that first drink of fresh water. After drinking all they wanted and making a meal of sorts off the birds, they pulled the canvas sail over their heads and settled down for the night.

In the morning they were reluctant to leave the fresh water, but the spot they were in was exposed to the full blast of the biting south wind and there was little wood to be found, so they knew they must push on and hope to find a more sheltered spot. They rolled up the canvas sail and were about to make a start when out of the long grass a man suddenly appeared. He let out a yell as he saw them and they recognized their Irish crewmate, Mickey (John) Grattan.

After the first exclamations of surprise, Mickey explained that he had changed his mind about staying behind and had followed them, but had not been able to find them. He was desperate for food, but even better was the fresh water they showed him. He plunged his head right in the pond and drank as if he would empty it. He was reluctant to leave it when they prepared to move on but went with them, cheerfully pointing out that at least there didn't seem to be any *"scorpions or serpents"* on the island.

At that time they had not seen any life at all on the island except for the mollymawks and the "night birds" as they called the shearwaters. They came at last, in the afternoon, to a sheltered valley.

It was the best they had found so far they all agreed. It was not far from the sea, and although there were no birds nesting nearby there was fresh water and plenty of scrubby wood for burning. They made camp feeling more cheerful than they had for days.

That night, though, it rained heavily again and the ground became so soggy that they found themselves sinking into it where they lay under a layer of wet canvas. They could find no way to get warm and dry. By morning they were so weakened by cold and hunger that, although they knew they should go back and tell their shipmates that they had found water, they just could not seem to make the effort.

"We had the heart but not the power," Charlie said.

They had reached that most dangerous point when they were so weak that they did not much care if they lived or died; they might well have just given up then, but out of the mist and driving rain staggered two figures, so exhausted they had to crawl the last few yards.

Daniel MacLaghlan and Harry Waters were barely recognisable, they looked so gaunt and ill. When the pair had recovered a little, they told their story.

They told how they had also found water, but the men were so weak from hunger, cold and being constantly wet, that they were hardly able to move. To make matters worse their fire went out and they were unable to light another. When they set out to follow the first party, arguing that they would no worse off, they had hoped Mr Peters would be able to manage with help, but they were only halfway up the mountain when he was forced to stop, unable to walk at all. They said the other men were coming on behind them, Karl Knudsen and Santiago Marino supporting Mr Peters.

As they talked the rest of the group straggled in – all but two. Mr Peters and Jack Puhze were not with them. Karl Knudsen explained that Mr Peters had lost the use of his legs entirely. They had built him a little hut with clods of earth and Jack had stayed with him. He was resting, Karl added, but they would go back for him even if they had to carry him every step of the way.

After they had rested and eaten, Karl Knudsen, Santiago Marino and three other men took a few cooked birds and set off to fetch him, but two days later – their twelfth day on the island – Karl returned to say that Mr Peters had died. They had wrapped him in a piece of sailcloth, buried him in a shallow sandy grave covered with a mound of turf and left him.

Their only consolation was that the First mate was out of his pain at last. Karl promised that one day they would see that he had a proper burial, but for now this was all they could do. They had made every effort they could to help the First Mate, but it had not been possible to keep him alive and every man grieved for him.

Mickey Grattan spoke for them all when he said that it was Mr Peters who had kept their hopes up ever since they had been thrown up on the bleak little island. Mr MacLaghlan was now the chief officer, but he was in a bad way, too.

"*We all were*", recalled Charlie.

Things could hardly have been much worse. For the most part, the men were dressed in thin trousers, torn to shreds, their shirts full of holes, their coats ragged and half of them had no socks or shoes. Their food was tough, fishy seabirds, seaweed and grass. They slept on the bare ground, their bodies sinking into muddy slush under a sailcloth coverlet with, as often as not, a layer of melting snow on top of it. If they had been able to salvage anything at all from the wreck they might have been better off, but the *Dundonald* was under water, all but her masts, and the sea was too rough to dive into.

It was April now. It would be spring in England, but there in the southern hemisphere the days were shortening and the weather could only turn colder as the winter approached. All they could do was take each day as it came.

Miraculously, no one else died. Mr Peters had been an older man and seriously injured, but the rest of them kept going somehow. Perhaps it was because they never quite gave up hope. If one man was low there was always someone else to give him a lift. There was always someone on look-out for passing ships – one day, surely, one would pass and see their smoke. They even caught a few mollymawks alive and attached scraps of sailcloth to their necks before releasing them, in the faint hope that someone, somewhere, would find their message. (No one ever did). Meanwhile, there on the horizon, when it was not hidden by mist, was the rocky shore of the main island.

April became May, then June, and as if their bodies had grown used to the harsh conditions, Charles Eyre says they actually grew stronger. He also described them *"a gaunt ragged set"* with *"thin fever-wasted faces and long, unkempt hair and beards"* and as *"miserable scarecrows"*. However, they do not seem to have suffered from scurvy, which would have been caused by a lack of vitamin C in their diet, possibly because of the seaweed they ate. Scurvy had once been the death of many seamen on long voyages until it was discovered that it could be prevented by improving their diet. James Cook insisted his men eat sauerkraut, even flogging any man who refused, and was proud that he never lost a man to scurvy.

The castaways found they could walk further, tackle heavier jobs, but one thing they all knew was that the worst of the winter was still to come. Their only shelter was still the canvas sail and while that kept the worst of the wind off them, there was no way they could have a fire beneath it. The cold would be a killer.

In his story, as told to Escott-Inman, Charles Eyre does not mention the Second Mate keeping a journal, but the Otago Witness, a weekly newspaper, carried a few extracts from such a diary in the edition published 4 December 1907, so it appears Daniel MacLaghlan must have had some kind of notebook and pencil on him when the wreck occurred which somehow survived a soaking.

"We have very few boots or socks," he wrote, *"and the weather is getting colder every day, so that we think we will die if the winter is severe. Our food still consists of young mollyhawks (sic) and cold water. We are beginning to see that we shall freeze to death if we live in our canvas camp during the winter."*

The published extract does not give us dates or show where the breaks come. It may have been a little later when he wrote, *"We are talking about* digging a hole in the ground, which is very soft and damp. We do not know whether it will be a success. So far we have not found a piece of wood big enough to make a shovel, but the third mate went over to the wreck, where he knew there was a piece of the foretopgallant-mast on the rocks, as it was there when we got the sail ashore. This piece being about 5in broad and 4ft long, came in useful for a shovel. A Russian who was living with the third mate knew something about building a mud cabin for pigs, as they used to make them at Home."

The 'Russian' was Michael Pul, from Estonia. Charlie's account is rather different, giving the credit for the idea to Mr MacLaghlan himself. He tells how they huddled around the fire discussing what to do, Mickey Grattan groaning that he was half frozen already. Everyone had their say.

They knew they were stuck there for at least a couple of months, for as Karl Knudsen pointed out, even if they could build a raft, the sea was too rough to make a crossing. They must wait until the worst of the winter was over

"We'll be dead by then!"

"If only we could find a nice big cave..."

"There isn't one on the entire island."

John Judge said they must try to build a cabin such as they had in the Old Country, no doubt thinking of his home in Ireland and the small cabins built by the peasants from slabs of peat. They all knew how the cabins had been built, but the windswept little island had neither the wood nor the peat they needed.

The other Irishman, Mickey Grattan, suggested it would have to be a very big cabin to hold them all, but Mr MacLaghlan said the idea was good and that the talk of a cave had reminded him of what the old earth-dwellers did in bygone days. They dug a hole in the earth and made a roof over it with reeds.

Mickey repeated it would have to be a big hole for them all.

According to Charles Eyre, Mr MacLaghlan went on to explain that they would need to dig a deep hole, place a long piece of wood across it and cover it with clumps of tussock. Possibly he was putting to them the idea that Michael Pul, with his limited English, had spoken of to him. The men were naturally doubtful. Charlie pointed out that they would not find a length of wood very easily, while another man wondered how they would dig down with no tools. The top layer of soil was soft from the rain, but as they went deeper it would become harder.

Once again Mickey was optimistic, if not very practical. They must dig with their nails like rabbits or moles, he said.

Charlie wished he had a rabbit then and his stomach growled with hunger at the thought..

Karl Knudsen was more realistic. Never mind talking about what they had not got, he said. Instead of building one big hut they must make a lot of small ones. They could work in pairs. It looks a big job to dig out six or seven feet of earth, but he was sure they could do it. Someone muttered that he should have been born a worm.

In spite of all the difficulties they raised, most of the men thought it was a good idea – and no one had a better suggestion – so they paired off and set to work. Mr MacLaghlan wrote, "we started digging a hole 6ft broad and 10ft long. The shovel was small but the ground was soft, and we succeeded in digging the hole, although it took some time as it was 4ft deep."

Later he wrote, "We have now been 55 days on the island, and we find the house a great deal better than was the canvas tent….. All the party, *seeing that the house is a success, divide into companies of two or three and start house building, and now there is a great demand for the shovel."*

Charlie and John Judge worked together. They decided they could manage with a space six feet by four feet. (two metres by one and a half) Generally speaking, the majority of people were shorter a century ago than the people of today. It would be small and cramped but it was only for sleeping in and anything bigger would be hard to keep warm. They made a start, scrabbling away with their bare hands but it wasn't long before their nails were broken and bleeding and they'd hardly scratched the surface.

At that rate they would be old men before they were finished, observed the pair.

Charlie remembered the road gangs he had seen mending the streets of London, breaking the surface with their pickaxes.

"Suppose we get pieces of wood to break the earth up a bit," he said.

They still had food to find and wood to gather to keep the fire burning, so they left the digging for then and while they foraged for firewood they looked for pieces tough enough to be used as digging sticks. They used them by driving the point of the stick into the ground – not too far for fear of breaking it – and working it about until it cracked the earth, then they lifted out the loosened the clods. The idea soon caught on and it wasn't long before all the men were doing the same – unless they were able to get the shovel, I imagine. The rain had cleared and they were racing to get the work finished before it returned.

It was hard work and not done in a hurry. The days were short at that time of year with only a few hours of daylight. They were busy from morning till night with digging, gathering firewood, catching and cooking mollymawks, but at least the exercise kept them warm. It took two weeks just to excavate the hole, but it was ready to be roofed at last, although it looked too much like a grave for Charlie's liking.

They found two sturdy pieces of wood, each forked at one end like a clothes prop used to hold up a washing line. They pushed these into the ground, one at the head and one at the foot of the 'grave' and hammered them well in for they were to support the long piece of wood that would run the length of the hut. Nowhere could they find a single piece long enough so they lashed two lengths together. Once again the rigging they had cut from the wreck came is useful.

Next came the pieces slanting from the ridge pole to the ground along the sides of the hole and on these they laid a network of lighter sticks, criss-crossed and interwoven like a basket. Finally, all that remained was to make the roof. They tore up bunches of long grass, piling it on a foot thick. This was covered with big tussocks, then a second layer of grass and last of all pieces of wood to prevent the wind from blowing it away. The work was done at last and they were proud of their new home.

Inside, however, they were ankle deep in liquid mud.

After some discussion, they decided to line it with yet more grass. First they lined the sides, driving wooden pegs into the earth sides, twisting a length of twine around one peg, then around a bundle of grass, around the next peg and so on until the sides were well covered. Then they cleared out as much of the soft mud on the bottom as they could before laying down a 'floor' of sticks covered with ferns, then grass, then more ferns and a final layer of grass. They found that a good strong twine could even be made from grass.

The house was complete. It was very dark inside and their feet sank into the soft floor. At one end they could stand upright – just – but at the entrance they had to crawl on hands and knees to get in. All the better to keep out the cold and wet, they agreed. It was snug and dry. In fact, you could almost call it cosy, especially after they built a low wall from clods of earth each side of the entrance to shelter it from the wind.

Daniel MacLaghlan's diary also mentions the water. They thought at first that it would make the house a failure, *"However, the water did not increase, although the ground kept damp."*

Now that they had houses, the canvas sails could be cut up to make clothing. Rough and ready trousers and jackets were hacked out with knives and cobbled together with threads of sailcloth or yarn unravelled from rope. They found that the fine bones of the mutton birds made good needles with one end rubbed to a sharp point and an eye pierced through the other end with a knife. Life was slowly becoming more bearable.

CHAPTER SIX

It was about the same time as the men finished making their huts, that two of them were away from the camp scavenging for firewood when they came to the edge of a very steep cliff, overhanging the shore. As they peered down at the tumble of rocks on the beach below, they were astonished to see some kind of animal moving about among the boulders. They must have been two of the younger, less experienced men – perhaps George Ivimey or the cabin boy Albert Roberts – for neither of them knew what the animal was.

They raced back to tell the others of their discovery and there was much discussion as to what it could be. Older hands like Mr Maclaghlan and Karl Knudsen said at once that it must be a seal. This caused huge excitement for where there was one, there must be more and seals meant real meat, far more nourishing than the seabirds which were all they had eaten for weeks. They were all gaunt and scrawny by then, slowly starving. Seals would also provide warm sealskin clothing instead of the rags and canvas they had shivered in until then.

Some of the men were all for rushing down to the beach right away before the seals departed, but the more experienced hands explained that seals were creatures of habit and would stay on their regular breeding ground for the season unless something scared them off.

The seals were actually Hooker's sea lions, the rarest today and fully protected.

The pair who had seen the seals warned that there was no easy way down to the beach, describing it as a 'nasty' place. That night they sat up late around the camp fire, talking over how best to tackle the business, determined to be up early in the morning to go and see the place for themselves.

Charlie's heart sank when he saw the massive bluff rising two hundred feet from the sea. The top overhung the lower part which had been worn away by the constant wash of the waves. What beach there was, was covered by a jumble of stones and large boulders that had fallen from the cliff over many years. Bob Ellis declared solemnly that no one could get down there.

The men were downcast; it looked truly impossible. Michael Pul pointed out a narrow ledge, like a groove cut into the cliff. It slanted across and down the face of the cliff to the beach. They had not noticed it at first for it was almost hidden by hanging moss, dripping with water from the overhang. It looked as dangerous as a path could be.

John Judge drew their attention to something moving down below them -- a seal was making its way with awkward, floppy jerks across the beach to the sea. It was a female with her pup following behind her. The men saw the seal only as mighty good eating, if only they could manage to get at it.

Charlie said that it was like the island they could all see – good if only they could reach it.

Michael Pul was still studying the rocky ledge, working out in his mind where it ran, where a man would have to jump or slide. He came to the conclusion that he could do it. In spite of all their protests that it was not possible, that he would be mad to even think of it, he insisted stubbornly that he was going to try. It was no worse than where he and Harry had climbed up from the wreck.

Harry Walters and Herman Querfeldt agreed that was true. The second Mate reminded them how Walter Low had fallen to his death, but Pul shrugged his shoulders, determined to try. A man could only die once, he said, adding that he could not stand seeing those seals down there and not try to get at them and that he thought the path was not as hard as it looked.

Harry Walters offered to go with him, but Pul refused to have anyone go with him saying there was no sense in risking two lives. If he was successful then others could follow him. None of them were happy about letting him take the risk; like the others, he was not the strong fit man he had once been. They even suggested drawing lots to see who should go, but Pul had made up his mind.

Armed only with a knife, he began his descent. They clustered at the top, hardly able to breathe for fear of seeing him fall. But he was cool and cautious as he made his way along and down, never lifting a foot until he had worked out where he was going to place it.

The men stared down at the beach. Now they looked more closely they could see seals all over the rocks. As they watched they saw many of the black 'rocks' move, rolling over to scratch lazily or flop towards the sea. They were indeed seals, so many that there was a good chance that Michael Pul would get one – if he made it down there of course. Mickey then asked how Pul was going to get a seal back up the cliff? It was a good point and Karl immediately sent someone back to camp for a rope.

Michael was still inching his way along the ledge. Then he was out of sight, hidden by the overhang. They waited in tense silence, giving a sigh of relief as he reappeared, clinging to the rock like a fly on a wall. Then they gasped as he slipped on the moss, but he hung on.

I can imagine they all agreed with Santiago when he said Pul was a brave man and he would succeed.

Michael disappeared again. The time seemed endless as they watched the spot at the bottom where they expected him to emerge. The tension became too much for Bob Ellis who suddenly declared that he was going down after Pul as he should have appeared by now unless he had had an accident.

As he spoke, Mickey Grattan spotted him on the beach and he let out, in Charlie's words, "a real Irish yell", loud enough to scare every seal for miles around. They hushed him quickly, but it was true – Michael was there. He looked up at Mickey's yell and waved.

Being from the far north, Michael had met with seals before. They were not to be taken lightly, he knew, and a bite from one of them would be a serious matter. Avoiding the large males that raised their heads, barking at him and looking as if they might attack, he loped across the beach to cut off a half-grown animal that was making a dash for the sea. He knew that if his prey reached the water he would lose it. Seals were clumsy on land, but swift and agile in the water. He drew near, getting between the seal and the water. He picked up a hefty piece of rock and as the animal barked and showed its teeth, he hurled the rock with all his might. It hit the seal, full on the nose, the only place where the rock would do any damage, stunning it instantly. Michael finished the job quickly and cleanly.

The men yelled down from above not to attempt the difficult climb carrying the seal, that they had sent for a rope. Michael could not make out the words so he waved and carried on skinning and gutting the carcass. He threw the entrails into the sea to keep the beach clean then rolled up the skin to be collected later. He cut off as much of the best meat as he could carry and began his climb. He arrived at the top at the same time as the rope.

It was a triumphant march back to camp where they made up a great glowing fire on which to roast thick slices of seal meat. I can only imagine the joyful satisfaction they experienced as they feasted. The meat was fat and oily but after the tough and fishy birds it tasted delicious. When they were all full and had licked their oily fingers and wiped their greasy chins, they made plans to return. They would pick up the skin and look at ways of making the path safer, too, and work out the best way to bring up the seals they caught.

It is illegal now and seems cruel to kill the endangered and gentle-eyed sea lions, but the lives of the crew depended on obtaining sufficient food and warm clothing to see them through the winter. It was literally the difference between life and death to them. By the middle of June the weather was at its worst with lashing rain every day and a sea so rough that there was scarcely a hope of sighting a sail coming to their rescue – not that that stopped them scanning the horizon constantly. At least the bitter cold kept the seal meat from spoiling.

They didn't waste a thing. The skins were stretched on rough frames, scraped as clean as they could get them and kept near the smoky fires for two or three days to dry. Sewing thread was picked out of the sailcloth. As seamen, they were used to mending their own clothing and now they turned their hands to making sealskin coats, trousers, caps and boots.

Michael Pul had worn moccasin-like 'slippers' on the farm where he grew up and now he showed the others how they were made from sealskin. Fur side out, the toes and heels were sewn, then holes pierced all around the top edge. A draw-string was threaded through the holes, pulled tight and knotted behind the heel. Strings were then crossed over the foot, under the instep and knotted on top. They soon wore out, lasting perhaps only two or three weeks, but were soft and warm.

The little shearwaters that they had thought too small to eat, besides being hard to find in their burrows, were now caught to make needles from their fine bones, piercing a hole in one end with the tip of a knife. They used the skins of the birds they caught, too, stitching them into feathery blankets and warm feathery 'socks' to wear inside the boots.

The fifteen men got along together pretty well considering how closely they lived with each other. Of course there were disagreements now and then, just as there are in every family, but rarely any serious quarrels. Everyone had little habits which were usually ignored but if they became too irritating the best thing to do, they found, was to change partners for a while.

Charlie had built his house with John Judge, but John was a quiet, thoughtful man and Charlie liked to talk. After a few nights they decided they'd be better friends if they did not have to live together, so Charlie moved into a slightly larger house with Second Mate Mr MacLaghlan and Harry Walters. Mr MacLaghlan, in particular, was always ready for a good discussion on any topic that was occupying Charlie's lively mind.

The little settlement was made up of five huts, each with its own fire that was never allowed to go out, and each little group of two or three men doing their own cooking in one of several cook houses they had built. These had shelves cut into the sides and a chimney at one end. There was also a store house for the meat which was kept off the ground by being hung on hooks made of forked sticks.

Catching and cooking the mollymawks was a big part of their day. Mr MacLaghlan tells how they would lift a young bird from the nest and if it was too light they would replace it, but if it was fat and heavy it became dinner. He describes the cooking of the birds – *"The birds being skinned, we begin cooking one for our meal, but as we consider no meal complete without a bit of fat we cook some on a stick that is called a greaser. There is always a lot of growling about mislaying the greaser. Everybody cooks his own bird, and when he has finished cooking he calls the next for cooking..... The birds are generally burnt on the outside and raw in the inside..... As it is not very pleasant cooking in the open, especially when it is raining and snowing, we started making a house for cooking. This house is similar to the others."*

The cook house was often very smoky and they would emerge well blackened with smoke. *"Having no soap, we have no means of washing, so we look like savages. However, a mollyhawk's (sic) skin is used for towel and soap. We rub our faces with the greasy part first, then wipe with the feather side. This is called a skin wash."*

I imagine the smell must have been overpowering, but as they all smelt the same after a while they would no longer have noticed it.

Some of the smoke seeped out through the grass roof. Quite by chance they discovered that leaving a bird on the roof turned the meat brown and made it far more tasty. After that they regularly smoked the birds.

They were always busy. They would set out each morning to catch about five or more birds each, which may sound a lot until you remember that there was no other food – no bread or vegetables or fruit. The young mollymawks were about the size of a large duck, the older ones the size of a goose. Then wood had to be gathered to keep the fire in and stock-piled, too, because the time might come when they were snowed up, unable to get out. Clothes and blankets had to be made and mended and the hut had to be kept clean and in good repair.

The last job each evening was to bank the fire down for the night. First they burned a great pile of green brushwood until there was nothing left but a heap of glowing ashes and the men were well-warmed through for the night. Then they laid two or three big pieces of wood, as thick as a man's arm, on the ashes, heaping the ashes over the wood. Next they placed large lumps of earth over the top, taking care to stop up any gaps where smoke was escaping.

"You'll put the fire out!" Charlie had protested the first time he saw this being done. He wanted to rush in and lift off the earth and let the air get to the fire. The next morning when the earth was removed all he could see was a low mound of grey, dead ash. As soon as this was raked away, however, there were the large lengths of wood, glowing red-hot. A few wisps of grass and dry twigs and the fire was blazing away merrily.

By managing disagreements, by keeping busy, following a routine, by lively discussion, the castaways kept up their spirits and were as healthy mentally as well as physically as could be expected in the harsh conditions. There was laughter, too.

One night the fire was banked as usual before Charlie and the other two crawled through the small entrance into their hut. They were soon asleep. Outside, a stray ember had somehow escaped being covered. The grass around it began to smoulder. Fanned by the wind, the flame grew brighter. It crept along the ground until it came to the grass walls and roof of the hut. It began to lick hungrily.

Charlie woke with a start to find himself being shaken violently by Mr MacLaghlan who was coughing and choking in the thick smoke that had filled the hut. From outside came shouts and yells as other people saw what was happening. It was already uncomfortably hot inside and sparks were dropping on him from above. Charlie yelled to Harry to get out quickly then scrambled for the exit to join the men beating frantically at the flames.

In all the excitement no one had noticed that Harry had not followed Charlie out. Suddenly his head burst up through the roof of the hut. He was blinking in confusion, his mouth opening and shutting, but what he was saying no one could hear and at that very moment Mr Maclaghlan brought his stick down, thwack! right on Harry's head, knocking him straight back into the burning hut again.

For a moment everyone was horrified, but before they could leap to his aid, a roar of rage was heard and out through the opening charged Harry, head first. He glared around, like a maddened bull. His eyes lit on Mr MacLaghlan and he roared again. Mr MacLaghlan took one look at Harry's face, threw away his stick and ran – with Harry in hot pursuit.

Of course the hut had to be completely rebuilt but every time the men remembered Harry's surprised face popping up and the sight of him charging after the Second Mate they would double up with laughter.

CHAPTER SEVEN

The evening, when they were gathered around the fire, was the time for discussions. Their hands were busy, whittling a wooden spoon, scraping a skin, sharpening a needle on a stone, or sewing a feather blanket or a skin garment. It might be a jerkin of two pieces joined along the top of the sleeves, under the seams and down the sides, no fastenings needed. While they worked they told yarns of strange things they had seen in other countries; they talked of their homes and always of food, but one topic never failed to come up sooner or later – how could they get off this tiny island?

Bob Ellis said they were better off staying where they were. They had fire and shelter there, he reminded them. Auckland Island was a big place. A bloke could wander about for days over there, trying to find the depot.

Charlie was not convinced. He knew they could not stay where they were forever, while Mickey Grattan moaned at the very thought; he did not want to stay there while there were all sorts of good things over the water if they could only get to them.

It was John Judge who warned them that they would have to go there eventually whether they liked it or not because the food would run out. This was something that had not occurred to Charlie. There were still plenty of birds, even though each man ate about five a day, necessary with no bread or potatoes to fill up their empty bellies, an average of seventy five birds a day.

But John Judge was speaking from experience. The birds would soon start to get scarcer. The young ones were getting their feathers. When they could fly they would leave the island and not return until the next breeding season.

Charlie admitted that he had not thought of that. It occurred to him then that the seals might not always be there either. They, too, would move on when the time came.

There was always 'root'," someone said glumly. This was a plant with large leaves and a fleshy root *"as long as a man's arm and a good deal thicker"* that they had found tasted a bit like turnip. They cooked it in the hot ashes of the fire. No one knew its real name so they simply called it 'root'. It was actually *Stilbocarpa Polaris*.

But John Judge's warning had brought them back to the old question. Mr MacLaghlan voiced it. *"How can we build a boat from the stuff that grows on this miserable island?"*

As Mickey Grattan said, there was not a scrap of wood to be found that did not sink like iron. They had not got the wood and they had no tools.

It was true; the wood was so heavy it would not float, as they had discovered, but that was not necessarily a problem. Mr Mclaghlan pointed out that iron was heavier than water, but ships were built of it.

"We didn't have tools to build our huts, but we built them," Charlie said.

But that had been solid earth they reminded him, not salt water. With fire they could shape wood and burn holes for wooden pegs in place of nails. They could hollow out the trunks of trees with fire. The same objection was raised again – there were no trees on the island to shape or hollow out, so what was the use of even talking about it?

Herman Querfeldt, meanwhile, had been working away quietly, making himself a canvas jacket. As he took off his old waistcoat, reduced to rags now, he felt something in the lining. He wriggled his fingers inside the tattered lining and pulled out six matches, little wax vestas, bent and broken but all with heads on them. They must have slipped through a hole in his pocket and dropped into the lining. You would have thought they were diamonds the way the men gathered round to see them.

They were wet, but it did not take long to dry them and then they were stored away in a little tin box someone had. They were the answer to one problem – how they would make fire if they got across to Auckland Island. The matches could make the difference between failure and success.

It always came back to that – reaching the main island. They had to cross that treacherous six mile (eight kilometre) stretch of water. The young birds were getting bigger and would soon be able to fly. The seals now recognized the danger the men posed and took to the water as soon as they sighted them.

"There's only one way I can think of," said John Judge. "We still have a good bit of canvas, even though it's cut up for clothes. Why not make a canvas boat? If we could gather a dozen or so pieces of wood, bent as near to right angles as we can find, it might be done."

Charlie says that when Judge came up with this suggestion there was an outcry of disbelief. A canvas boat? Who would risk their life in such a fragile craft?

What Judge was proposing was to construct a coracle. Coracles had been built in Wales and by the people along the river Severn in England for over a thousand years. They were small oval boats, made by stretching skins or, later, canvas, tightly over a frame of willow, coating it thickly with pitch (tar) to make it water tight. The men would almost certainly have at least heard of them, but were unlikely to have any experience of constructing or rowing one.

It was not surprising that some men did not care for the idea of taking a flimsy canvas boat to sea. They were none of them cowards, but the sight of the great rolling waves breaking far out then rushing, hissing and seething on to the shore, must have made them quake. How could they launch a boat into that? Few if any of them could swim. And was the shore on the far island any better or was it, too, a mass of boulders and jagged cliffs? They would have to be crazy to even try.

However some of the men, Charlie among them, declared it was the best idea so far, risky though it was. He had been shaken by the thought that the food might run out. Anything was better than starvation.

"Nothing venture, nothing have,' as he put it. "Starvation is staring us in the face. It is only death a little sooner if the worst comes to the worst."

The next day they abandoned their sewing and spread out in small parties to search for anything that might be used for the framework of a canvas boat. But for all their searching they found nothing suitable. There seemed to be nothing. Some of them sighed at the thought of the timber from the *Dundonald* which had all drifted away, but it would have been impossible to work with no carpentry tools.

Then one day Santiago Marino found something he thought might just do. Wandering in search of firewood, he came across some strange tangled shrubs he had not seen before. Season after season the blustering winds had curled and twisted them into every fantastic shape imaginable – anything but straight - until they were tangled like a nest of writhing snakes. When he pulled at it he found the wood was light, but very tough. He marched back to camp with a piece of it on his shoulder.

"What have you got there, Santiago?" Charlie called out.

"Piece wood," he shouted. He was from Chile, nick-named the Black Prince due to his dark colouring, and his English was limited.

John Judge, the acknowledged expert on coracles, examined the piece Santiago had brought. It was hard, dark wood, bent in the middle somewhat like a boomerang, twisted and knobbly and thorny. He did not know what wood it was - it was actually a variety of hebe, *veronica elliptica* – but his face lit up. If they could find a dozen pieces bent like that they would be well on the way to making their boat!

At first they thought he must be mistaken and meant straight, but Judge said not at all. If they stripped off all the side twigs and tied the ends of two pieces together they would have a long straight piece turned up at each end. That would be the keel of the boat and more of the same across it would make the ribs. If they wove smaller branches in and out they would have a frame to stretch the canvas over. He urged them to 'buck up' and go and search for more pieces like this.

Suddenly seeing what John Judge meant, they followed Santiago Marino to where he had made his find. Every piece they picked up was examined for splits and tested for strength. A sudden break at sea could be the death of every man in the boat. The selected pieces were smoothed as much as possible by scraping and burning; they did not want to risk damaging their precious knives on the hard wood. Meanwhile other men carefully unravelled lengths of rope. When all was ready they began to lash the pieces of wood together, two by two, testing every knot to be sure it was as tight as it could be made.

Charlie thought it looked like a loosely woven basket, just about long enough for him to lie down in – not that he'd fancy stretching out on anything as lumpy and knotty as that! He shook his head. He must be mad to even think of trusting his life to such a rough and ready contraption.

They spread out the canvas they had left. It was in a sorry state from mud and rain, hacked about where they had cut into it for clothes, but there was enough left to cover the frame. They cobbled it on tightly with great rough stitches, dragging the strands of rope through the tough canvas with the strongest of their bird-bone needles. They needed palm pads to protect their hands as they forced the sharp bones through the canvas.

There it was – nothing more than a canvas-covered basket really. There were no planks or seats inside. Whoever ventured out in it would have to kneel on the rough, knobbly wood. There would be no changing places once they had set out – there would be no room for that – and they would have to be very careful not to knock holes in the bottom.

By now June was ended and July brought bitter cold with snow, sleet and storms day after day. Their clothing was roughly made and definitely smelly, but thanks to the seals, it kept them warm, especially the sealskin boots. They were not the fit men they once had been, but they all felt stronger and could walk for miles without becoming exhausted. Surely they were fit enough now to attempt the crossing?

There was only one place suitable for launching the coracle. It was directly opposite the island they wanted to reach, so on 28 July they carried the little boat down to the water. They held their breath until, with immense relief, they saw that she actually floated and what's more, did not leak too badly, although someone would have to bail constantly.

What about oars? That was the next question.

These were made from the longest straight pieces of wood they could find that were forked at one end. Over the fork they stretched more canvas, sewing it on firmly, lashing the handle round and round. They had their paddles.

The boat was ready, but the weather was blowing hard, whipping up the sea so that there was no chance of setting off yet. With three men in it, the coracle was so deep in the water that there were only a few inches of freeboard. It was hard to be patient. The men were sure that all the food and clothing they needed were just waiting for them on the big island.

The next decision was who was to go? The tiny craft would only carry three, two to row and one to bail. Some men said straight out they would rather stay where they were than risk certain death. Some wanted to go but were shouted down on the grounds that they were not strong enough. The discussion went on for the best part of a day before it was agreed that Santiago Marino, Bob Ellis and Michael Pul should be the ones. Plans were made.

They would need fire when they landed. The fires around the houses were never allowed to go out, so it was decided that they must take Herman Querfeldt's six vestas. They promised to take the greatest care of the matches and not to use a single one more than was absolutely necessary. They were told to light a fire as soon as they landed and to make as much smoke as possible so their shipmates would know they had made the crossing safely.

It was agreed that there was no need to take any food, apart from a little cooked mollymawk to eat on the way, because they were confident that there would be plenty of birds over there, and water too, until they found the depot.

The last day of July dawned. The wind had gone. The sea was calm. Suddenly all was bustle and excitement. Who knew how long the good weather would last? Down to the beach they hurried and pushed the little boat into the water. It looked tiny. Michael Pul stepped in cautiously, then Santiago and Bob Ellis. They were handed the paddles. There was a pause, every man there made solemn by the importance of the moment.

Then, 'Cast off' came the command.

The men on shore gave a cheer.

"Good luck, mates!" they called. "God bless your journey!"

Half kneeling, half crouching, they worked their clumsy paddles. Bobbing low in the water they were carried swiftly out to sea and around the headland until they were out of sight. Then those on land raced to the top of the cliff to watch from there until all they could see was a speck in the distance. Charlie glanced at the sky. The sun was climbing higher. He thought they ought to make land about midday.

The atmosphere must have been tense. No one could settle to work. They wandered around camp, too restless to think of anything but their mates in that tiny boat. As the sun reached its highest point they could not keep their eyes off the distant island, hoping every minute to see the column of smoke that would mean all had gone well.

But no signal was sighted. The afternoon wore on; evening came and still no smoke. Darkness fell. The men whispered their worst fears. They must have gone down. The boat was not strong enough. She never made it.

Morning dawned, but still not a wisp of smoke was to be seen.

"We drank, reckless of what would follow, so long as our thirst was quenched."

"The seal turned, barking and showing its teeth."

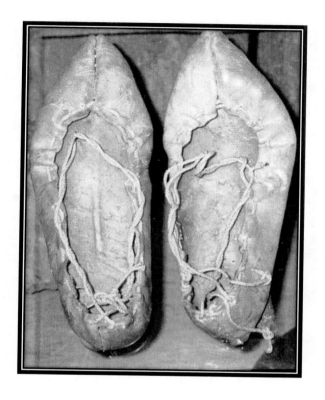

Sealskin slippers made by the crew of the *Dundonald*

"All in Vain! Dimmer and dimmer in the failing light the vessel grew."

"Then we went down and washed ourselves solemnly; we cut each other's hair and beards."

Crew members of the Dundonald posing with the framework of their coracle.

"We just behaved like so many madmen."

Crew of the Dundonald posed in front of their flagpole.
Erebus Cove depot, Auckland Island.

Left to right

Back row: Michael Pul, Bob Ellis, Mickey (John) Grattan, John Judge, Alfred Finlow, Harry Walters.

Middle row: Charles Eyre, John Stewart, Daniel MacLaghlan, Albert Rogers, Karl Knudsen (seated).

Front row: Jan Putze, Santiago Marino, George Ivimey, Herman Querfeldt.

"Survivors of the Dundonald wreck aboard the Hinemoa with the frame of their coracle."

Clockwise : Mickey Grattan, Bob Ellis, Michael Pul, Karl Knudsen.

A collection of photos taken by E.A.Phillips relating to the wreck of the Dundonald in 1907.

Clockwise from left top : A group of survivors with Mr Hutton,

Centre: George Ivimey with seal skins.

Top right: A group of visitors aboard the Hinemoa at Bluff.

Bottom right: A group of the survivors with the coracle aboard the Hinemoa.

Bottom left: The frame of the coracle.

CHAPTER EIGHT

The days that followed were among the hardest they had experienced. All the men were hungry. Charlie Eyre and Mickey Grattan spent an entire morning hunting for mollymawks but captured only three between them. The breeding season was over and the birds were deserting the island. The seals, too, had gone. The outlook was grim if they were to be reduced to eating baked 'root' for every meal. It was better than seaweed but hardly enough to keep the men alive through the bitter winter without some meat to go with it.

It seemed certain that the brave crew of three in the first boat had perished, but still the castaways scanned the horizon a dozen times a day. Hope died hard – and there had been reason to hope for a short time, for on 7 August, three days after the coracle had set off, a cry went up.

"Smoke!"

It was true. A cloud of dense grey smoke was billowing skyward before being dispersed by the southerly wind. Michael Pul, Bob Ellis and Santiago Marino must have reached the main island. They were alive after all, though no one could guess why it had taken three days for them to send up a signal.

Every man dropped what he was doing and rushed to help build up a great pile of wood on the cliff top to signal back. When it was well alight they smothered it with grass, damping it down so that it made thick smoke. They kept it going, but the fire on the distant island soon died down and there was no other sign of life over there, nor the next day or the next.

Some men were sure that if they had found a supply depot there would be a boat there. Others insisted that only stores, not boats, were left at the government depots, in which case the trio would have to return in their little canvas coracle and it would take many trips to carry everyone across, even if the weather allowed it. It became urgent to build more boats. They began to scour the island for more suitable pieces of *veronica elliptica*.

Before long the frames of two more coracles were completed and were ready to have their canvas stretched over them. They were a little bigger than the first boat had been and each would hold four men. There had been arguments about making them, some men saying they would never risk going to sea in them, others insisting that they had no choice – it was go or starve. Charlie made up his mind that when the new boats were finished he would get a place in one of them.

They were running out of canvas. It was a struggle to straighten out what they had, all folded and rolled up as it was, and they had no choice but to start unpicking the clumsy stitches on trousers and jackets, taking them apart and re-cobbling them into covers for the boats. They would manage without coats, they said, if it meant reaching the island and the depot of stores they were sure was there.

Then, after three more days, on 10th August, another column of smoke was spotted.

Why were they signaling again? Were they signaling that they were coming back, the men must have wondered? They rushed to the cliff top, and there in the distance was a small black object, coming gradually closer and closer until they could make out three figures paddling, their arms moving slowly, wearily. Their heads were low, their shoulders slumped. The watchers grew impatient, afraid that it would be dark before they made land, saying if they were as keen to see them as they were to see the rowers, they would put their backs into it!

Everyone made their way together down to the landing spot from where the coracle had left ten days before. The boat came nearer. Charlie said they looked dog tired. The rowers did indeed look completely done in.

"'They are beaten!' That was the thought that was pressing itself home upon us. Whatever story we were to hear, it would be one of failure; and we nerved ourselves to bear our disappointment like men."

Still there was some hope. A cheer went up when people saw that they had proper oars for that meant they must have found the depot.

The men in the coracle raised a feeble ghost of a cheer in reply, but when the craft grounded at last it was clear that the paddlers were so stiff, weary and wracked with cramp that they could hardly move. They were lifted out, barely able to walk. The coracle was pulled safely above the high water line and then everyone made their way back to camp, bombarding the three adventurers with questions every step of the way. What was it like over there? Had they found the depot?

Bob Ellis answered them.

"Ay, we reached the island and you ought to go down on your knees and thank God that you were cast away here and not over yonder. You can't live there, boys -- it's a deadly place. There is valley after valley of thick bush which no mortal soul can possibly penetrate. For pity's sake don't stop yarning here! Get us back to the camp and give us some water and food for we are almost done. I never wanted anything so much in all my life as a good chunk of root and a fat mollymawk."

In the fading light, the men began to take in what they had not noticed in their first excitement – the cuts and scratches on every limb, the clothes torn to rags, the complete exhaustion in their drawn, grey faces.

Gradually, after they had been fed and rested, they told their story. Bob Ellis did most of the talking since neither Michael Pul nor Santiago Marino were fluent in English. It was a grim story.

It was a hard row against the currents, Bob told them, and a risky job making a landing when they got there, but they made it. They pulled the boat up high and made their way north east up a sort of valley to see if they could find the depot. It was hard going from the first. The ground was so thick with thorny brushwood it just about sliced them to pieces. They were cut and bleeding and their clothes torn to ribbons even on that first day. Nevertheless they pushed on and made it to the top of the valley and then it started to rain in torrents.

A thick mist came down so they could see nothing. They had expected to find birds but there was not a single bird there. All they had to eat was what they had taken with them. Bob said they did not feel too downhearted at first. After all, they had reached their destination, now they were confident they would find the depot and then there would be all the food they could want.

They slept in the open that night. It was no use trying to light a fire with everything soaking wet in the heavy rain. They thought matters would improve in the morning, but when morning came the rain kept on and the mist was so thick they could not move more than a few steps without losing sight of each other. They kept heading north east as best they could judge in the conditions and were a good way from the sea, but still they had not sighted any depot or a hut or anything to eat. They were sick with hunger. It could not have helped that the three men were of different nationalities and could barely understand each other, yet they kept their nerve and pushed on. There was not a sign of life anywhere, just the rain falling, dripping, the rustle of leaves and the squelch of their feet.

No one said a word. They were too weary and dispirited.

That night, desperate for some warmth, they managed to light a fire, but it took two of their precious matches and in the morning they had to abandon it for they had no way of carrying it with them. They turned back the way they had come, sure they would have starved to death if they had continued on.

They had gone some way when they heard a noise, then out of the bush burst a wild boar. It *"stood looking at them in mingled surprise and defiance, and showed more disposition to fight than to flee,"* as Bob put it. A wild boar is a highly dangerous animal and according to Charles Eyre the three men were unarmed, although they must have had at least one knife, but the men were starving and the sight of all that food was all they needed to find the courage to jump the beast. They dragged it down, receiving some nasty gashes doing it, and finished it off. The boar was food for three days.

They were back in the valley near their landing site by then. They had to light another fire and that took two more matches. No one needed reminding that now only two remained. They guessed their crew mates would be looking out for a signal so they made the smoke which had been seen. They knew they would have to keep this fire in at all costs, so they left Santiago Marino to look after it while Bob Ellis and Michael Pul tramped to and fro, here, there and everywhere, looking for that depot in horrible conditions, getting even more scratched and bruised.

While he waited, Santiago kept busy, foraging around for wood to keep the fire going. He found some wreckage from the *Dundonald* washed up on the shore, carried across by the current. He carved out the two oars they used to come back with while he guarded the fire. Both were about five feet long.

They spent six days searching. They built a little hut for shelter, but still not a sign of a depot did they find and not another thing to eat. By then they were starving again. They thought of the men back on the small island, the houses they had built and the fires for warmth. They made the decision to return at once while the weather was fine. If the weather turned foul they could find themselves stranded there, starving. They made another smoke signal to warn that they were coming and launched off once more in the coracle. They had been gone ten days.

Some of the men listening still insisted that the depot must be there, and while others shook their heads and said they had known all along how it would turn out, they declared that another attempt must be made. Charlie Eyre was among those set on trying again in spite of Bob Ellis's words.

"You do as you like," growled Ellis. *"You will soon be glad enough to come back again. You don't catch me going to that hell hole anymore."* And *both Pul and the Chilean nodded agreement.*

No one doubted that every word was true. The men looked grimly at each other. Charlie could see from their faces that, like his, their hearts had sunk as the tale unfolded. But the depot *was* there! It *had* to be found! Another try *had* to be made!

The camp was divided evenly between those who said nothing on earth would make them attempt the crossing after what they had just heard and those, Charlie among them, who felt they had no choice. The birds had almost all gone, seals were scarce and although they were always on the watch for a passing vessel they knew no ship was going to come looking for them.

They set to work to finish the two new boats. It was agreed that it would not be wise to use the first one again. After the stress the framework had been under it could well break up half way across, but they stripped off the canvas to use again. By 20th August the new, larger boats were ready and the weather, although marginal, was fair enough to launch them for a sea trial. All went well.

Charlie said they must plan the trip properly and take food since there was none there. Karl Knudsen, who was as keen to go as Charlie, said they must take fire too. That was a problem. There were only two matches left and Herman Querfeldt had reclaimed them in case the fires in camp should by some misfortune be extinguished. But Charlie thought he knew a way round this, a way to carry fire with them in the boat. Just for now, though, he was keeping it to himself.

Charlie, Karl Knudsen, Mickey Grattan, Harry Walters and Second Mate Daniel MacLaghlan were all keen to go, but now the weather turned nasty again. Lashing rain, sleet, mountainous seas and gale force winds made any hope of setting off out of the question. It was hard to wait now the boats were ready, especially as food was becoming more of a problem with every day that passed.

On the fifth day, making their daily check that the boats were safe at the launching area, Charlie and Karl spotted a lone seal which they managed to catch. As usual, they cleaned the carcass on the spot and carried the entrails down to the shore to dump them in the sea. On the way back they noticed the trunk of a tree, just a bare dead stump, standing all alone a little way off - and that was odd because so far they had not seen a single tree on the island. It seemed a strange place for a tree to grow and was oddly flat on top.

They decided to take a closer look at it. It stood about six feet tall and was about the thickness of a lamp post. It was not a tree at all but a man-made post. After a bit of heaving and yanking, out the post came. The end had been sharpened to a point, they found. It was the first sign any of them had seen that another human being had ever set foot on Disappointment Island. Who had he been? What had become of him? Was the post some kind of sign or marker? If anything had ever been attached to it the weather had long since destroyed it.

The two men dug down with sticks, but although they cleared quite a big hole they found nothing but stones and soil. It remained a mystery.

The treacherous weather seemed to be deliberately tormenting them. For an hour or two the wind would drop and the sun would shine, but then, just as they were hoping that this would be the day, the wind would come howling back bringing rain, sleet and snow – and Heaven help any boat caught out in that!

They occupied themselves as best they could, gathering wood, hunting birds – although with little success – and repairing their clothes, but their spirits were low. They all had their down days, even the usually optimistic Charlie. As he said, *"Even I found it hard work to keep up my spirits, whilst Mickey's jokes were few and far between."* He crept off to be alone in his hut for a while. He lay there *"thinking sadly of those dear ones in far-away England, who long before this would have given me up for dead."* He was right. The *Dundonald* had long since been posted as missing on the Lloyds register, given up as lost and gone.

The sun was low in the sky and still he did not move, so deep was his depression, until suddenly a chorus of yells rang out.

"A ship! A ship! Sail-ho! Sail-ho!"

Charlie made a dive for the door. Outside men were rushing to and fro like madmen, jumping up and down, waving, yelling, falling to their knees with hands clasped in prayer, laughing, crying. There it was, a barque with her sails furled in the savage wind, sailing straight towards them. It was what they had hoped and prayed for since the day the *Dundonald* was wrecked.

Men were shouting out for a fire to be lit. Charlie snatched up a whole armful of wood and piled it on to his fire which had been allowed to die down to a mass of glowing embers ready for banking for the night. They piled on so much wood that they were in danger of putting it out, but it caught and soon bright flames were roaring up, turning the smoke pink and purple before it rose in a thick, dark column towards the sky.

As the sun sank lower, the dusk turned the sea grey and the flames flared higher and more vivid than ever. How could those on board the ship help but see them? Soon, at last, they would be rescued.

Then a groan of anguish and disbelief broke from their mouths. "No!" She was turning away! She couldn't be! But she was. The men howled and pleaded and cursed. Their fire lit up the night sky, showers of sparks floating up in the billowing smoke, but the ship grew smaller and smaller until she was a mere speck that faded and was gone.

The castaways were in utter despair after such hope and now such bitter disappointment. They fell into a stunned silence.

After a while they tried to cheer each other up, saying they must have been seen, they could not have been missed. They speculated that the other ship would come back for them or that they would report the sighting and then a Government vessel would be sent to pick them up. That would be better than risk running on to the rocks in the dark. The crew said that if they had seen one ship they might see others. The weather would start improving soon.

When it did, they would attempt the crossing, suggested Charlie, but Bob Ellis shook his head. He told them he was not going again. He was going to wait and keep his eyes skinned for another vessel, sure that there would be one soon.

It seems incredible that their fire had not been seen, but equally so that a ship would have ignored it. Charlie reports, "*So far as I can learn no vessel ever reported having seen our signal fire; and yet if they did not see it they must have been blind, for it must have been visible for miles – at least the glow and reflection must have, even if the flames themselves could not be seen. But she took no notice; she sailed off and we were left there as nearly frantic with despair as ever men could be.*"

CHAPTER NINE

Day after day went by. No rescue vessel came for them. No other ship passed the island. The weather remained bad and the sea between Disappointment Island and Auckland Island ran high and fierce. Time and again they returned empty handed after hunting for birds or seals. They were existing on 'root' or chewing grasses although these often made them sick with stomach cramps. Soon they would become too weak to row even when the weather finally improved.

One day in September, with the wind blowing a gale, blasting flurries of snow into their faces, Charlie decided there was nothing to do but try the seal beach again. He knew the seals only lay on the rocks when it was fine. Then they liked to sprawl lazily in the sun, but in bad weather they stayed at sea or hid away in holes among the boulders. Not that he was going to risk going in after one; that would be an invitation to have his head crunched. The only way was to poke at the hole with a long stick until the animal was enraged enough to come rushing out into the open. Then, if a man was quick enough, he stood a chance of getting a dinner. Charlie outlined his plan. It was met with little enthusiasm.

In that weather? It was not fit for dogs! They would rather be hungry than killed. The way down the cliff, under the overhang, was difficult even in good weather. They advised Charlie to wait as it might be better the next day. Charlie retorted that they had been saying that every day for weeks. A man could starve waiting for the sun to shine.

The crew told him he would never get down there and even if he did he would not find any seals and then if he did he would never get it back up the cliff. Charlie was still determined to go. As he told them, they had faced a great many things that seemed impossible but managed to do them somehow, so then Bob Ellis said he would go as well. He did not think they would have any luck, but Charlie would stand no chance alone. They would both be killed predicted the others.

"You keep the fire up and we'll get the seal," promised Charlie.

Perhaps it was the thought of the roasting meat that made Jack Stewart suddenly offer and then John Pulze said he would go as well, so the four of them armed themselves with sticks and set off.

It was a nightmare of a job, inching down the cliff, hanging on by their finger tips as their feet slipped on the wet moss while the wind swept up the face of the cliff and tried to drag them off it. Down below, the waves came rolling in like thunder, crashing in a cloud of spray on the rocks.

Once down they clambered among the huge boulders that littered the beach, slipping on the weed, always on the lookout for hidden gaps and holes into which they could so easily slip and break a leg or crack their heads or become jammed tighter than a cork in a bottle. There was not a seal to be seen.

John Pulze thought the sea too rough for the seals to come ashore but Charlie, working his way along the beach, hoped that it was this same rough weather that was keeping them in their holes.

Jack Stewart had been watching the tide rising. There was only a six foot stretch of land between the cliff and the water at high tide. He was uneasy. It would not do to be caught there when a big wave came crashing up to the foot of the cliff, snatching their feet from under them and washing them off the beach.

Charlie peered down a long narrow tunnel between two rocks.

"Grr-ough!"

A warning bark came back at him. He spotted a pair of eyes glowing in the dark and then a second pair. In fact there were four young seal pups holed up there. He would have to be quick. The tide was nearly in.

Glad that his stick was a long one, Charlie tried to dislodge the animals, all the while ready to jump clear if they rushed out. They clustered at the end, growling and biting at the stick, the tide coming higher all the time. After half an hour he was about ready to give up, when suddenly, without a moment's warning, all four seals rushed out together, straight at Charlie. Yelling a warning to Bob, he threw himself to one side. Bob was ready; a single whack on the vital spot on the nose was enough. One escaped but they had three young seals and starvation was held at bay for a little longer.

It was the end of September before a break in the weather came, a lull when they thought they could risk a crossing to Auckland Island. The seal meat was long gone and they were back to chewing 'root' and seaweed. They were ready to try anything to fill their empty bellies.

Meanwhile preparations had been made ready for the day when they could set out. There was a canvas bag for water that oozed a little but not too much, some cooked food and there was Charlie's fire-carrying invention. This was a large clod of earth with a hole scooped out of it and lined with stones. Glowing embers were put into the hole and they planned to carry small pieces of wood to feed it on the way.

Eight men had been chosen to go. In one boat were Karl Knudsen, Mr MacLaghlan, Mickey Grattan and young George Ivimey. In the other were John Judge, Harry Walters, Albert Roberts the cabin boy and Charlie himself. Karl Knudsen was worried, convinced that neither Albert nor George, the two youngest members, were strong enough and Mr MacLaghlan, an older man, was not fit for much. They all insisted they were up to it and reluctantly he gave in. As third officer on the Dundonald, he was next to Daniel McLaghlin in command.

"*Coats off, mates!*" Charlie called. The coats were too bulky to row in but they would help pad the sharp, knotty frame that dug painfully into their knees. Karl launched his boat first, alone. It handled well so Charlie pushed his out into the water. John Judge and Harry Walters stepped in and reached for the water bag, the fire and their coats.

Charlie eyed the waves rolling in – not crashing breakers but a big swell that lifted the fragile coracles and dropped them in a froth of surf that hissed over the rocky shore. Well, it was no use waiting for perfect calm. They must go while they could. Everything was in now and some of the men who were staying behind hung on to the rope while Charlie and Albert prepared to climb in.

At that very moment a monster of a wave came surging up the tiny inlet from the sea.

Look out! The warning shout came too late. Before the pair in the boat could drop the things they were stowing and seize the paddles, the wave had taken the tiny boat and sent it smashing on to the rocks, ripping the canvas and flipping the boat upside down. It disappeared under the water. The backwash dragged John Judge and Harry Walters with it and for a few minutes they were struggling for their lives. By the time their mates had dragged them out of the surf they were half drowned. The others hauled on the rope to try to drag the broken wreck to shore so that at least the canvas could be salvaged.

Meanwhile their precious coats were floating out to sea. Alone in the first boat, Karl made a grab for them, nearly capsizing his own craft in the process.

"*Come back in! Come in!*" Charlie yelled, seeing that with two men rowing, the coats might yet be saved. Karl turned towards the shore, fighting to keep the coracle from getting side on to the wind which was increasing in strength every minute.

As soon as he reached the beach Charlie scrambled in with him and seized an oar, yelling at him to get moving. They had to get those coats back somehow.

By now the coats had been tossed around by the waves and had drifted apart. It took almost an hour of hard paddling to retrieve them but they managed it at last and made it back to shore with them. Then Charlie and Karl beached the boat safely and went to see what, if anything was left of the other.

Their hearts sank as they surveyed the mangled wreckage. They had expected the frame to be smashed but to their dismay the canvas was shredded beyond repair. No amount of patching and painful stitching with their bird-bone needles would mend it now.

Charlie, trying as always to look on the bright side of things, said well at least they still had one boat. Karl said in a voice of absolute certainty, that he was not going anywhere that day and not going at all with the crew that was picked for him. They were not strong enough. He said he would not have agreed to go in the first place without Charlie and Harry and now their boat was gone he was not taking the risk.

Clearly there was no point in arguing. When they asked what he intended to do, he said he was going back to camp. They had nearly drowned two men and lost one boat through not waiting until the weather was right.

It was hard to give up but Knudsen was correct. In any case, they were too exhausted to do any more. They trudged home under clouds that were gathering for another storm.

Around the camp fire the discussion began again, covering much of the same old ground. What should they do? Try again of course. It was too risky. They would starve if they did nothing. Who should go? The boat would only hold four.

There was still the first little boat, but that would leave nothing for those left on the island. They would have no way of leaving if they had to later – although no one could say when that might be or what might happen to make it necessary.

Karl reminded them of what he had said already. He was not going unless he had a strong crew; strong enough to row and strong enough to survive when they got there. This was clearly essential after the experience of the three who had made the first crossing.

In the end it was agreed that another attempt must be made but that Karl Knudsen should be allowed to choose his own crew. He respected Mr MacLaghlan but the Second Mate was sick and sixteen year old George Ivimey was not strong either.

George was none too happy at losing his place, but Mr MacLaghlan said, *"You are skipper of that boat, so name your crew."*

Charlie Eyre commented to Escott-Inman, *"Of course, Knudsen was not really skipper, for we had long ago started to share alike, no one having any authority unless it was due to his personal strength of character. For instance, both Ellis and Knudsen were strong men; and somehow I always found that my advice was regarded thoughtfully, but I expect that was to a great extent due to my good spirits – I and Mickey Grattan kept the fellows lively."*

From among those wishing to go, Knudsen named Harry Walters, Charlie Eyre, and Mickey Grattan as three men who had proved themselves fit and resourceful.

Those who had made the trip before repeated their warnings that it was all madness and they would be only too glad to come back once they had seen what it was like over there, but Charlie thought it was no use listening to tales of gloom and despair. They must go just as soon as the weather permitted for all the birds were gone and they were near to starvation. He occupied himself with preparing another clod of earth to carry fire when that time came and this time he took extra care and found a flat stone to cover it and another piece of turf to lay on top of that.

At last, on 7 October, they woke to find the wind had dropped, the sea was calm and the sun was shining. This time surely they would get away.

CHAPTER TEN

It must have been in the minds of all the men that this was their last chance to reach the main island and the provisions they needed so urgently. I can imagine the care Charles Eyre took as he carefully scooped fresh hot ashes into his portable fire carrier, laid green wood on them and placed the cover he had made on the top. Two cooked birds – the last two remaining – were all the provisions they had. They had just two matches, the last two, that Herman Querfeldt had given them after all. As the light grew stronger they carried the boat down to the water. This time only two or three men came to see them off and hand them the fire, the food, the water bags and their coats (was it too early in the morning or had the others lost hope?) but they raised a small brave cheer as the four men pushed off and began to paddle. They were on their way.

Ahead of them lay Auckland Island. Charlie looked back at Disappointment Island. It was growing hazy already, but what a grim, black place it looked. It had been their home for seven months.

Midway between the two islands a stiff little breeze sprang up, making choppy waves that slopped over into the boat which only had five inches of freeway. In the bows Mickey Grattan was kept busy, bailing non-stop, while amid-ships Karl Knudsen and Harry Walters paddled. Someone had made a drinking vessel from sealskin, the shape held out by wire sewn around the rim, but this made a useful bailer. Charlie was at the stern with another paddle, using it as a rudder to keep them on course.

The coracle was a little over two metres long, (between six and eight feet) and about a metre (three feet) wide; not much room for four men. In spite of the coats, the pain in their legs as they knelt in the cramped little vessel was bad, but soon the pain in their arms and shoulders became worse – like red hot knives stabbing them while their hands were raw and blistered from the friction of the paddles. They would have given anything for the chance to rest, but if they had stopped their forward momentum would have been lost and they would have been swept sideways by the current, swamped and capsized within minutes. Karl never eased up for a moment and his sheer determination gave strength to the others.

They were nearing the coastline. The sun was high so they guessed it must be almost midday. They closed in making for the bay that Bob Ellis, Michael Pul and Santiago Marino had told them was the best landing place. When they saw it they were appalled, but there was no other place. All along the coast were tremendous cliffs, almost vertical, undermined in places by the pummelling of the sea.

When they saw the size of the waves breaking on the shore there, they were horrified, convinced the coracle would be smashed to smithereens. The bay was a froth of white water for a full quarter mile out to sea as it surged over submerged rocks and reefs. Beyond the reefs they could see a narrow shingle beach with a solid wall of trees rising up the hillside behind it.

But Mickey and Harry were exhausted. They could go on no longer. They would have to risk it.

They made for a break between two reefs but the swell was huge and they were forced to pull back. In a wooden boat they might have chanced it but not in the little coracle. The canvas would be shredded, the fragile frame shattered. If they lost the boat how would they ever get off again?

The weather was growing rougher by the minute, the wind wilder, the waves bigger; they certainly could not stay where they were. And then they saw it – a huge roller racing towards them. Karl shouted to them to go with it, to be quick before the next one swamped them.

"Now!" yelled Charlie as the roller crashed past them, breaking into a mass of foaming surf. Muscles on fire, they paddled for their lives. Charlie steered for the least jagged part of the beach. Over his shoulder he could see the next wave bearing down on them and shouted to Mickey to stand by ready to jump.

Mickey Grattan, in the bow, grabbed hold of the rope, determined to hang on to it at all costs. Then the wave caught them, lifting them up and forward and dashing them down on to submerged rocks close to shore. Mickey leaped ashore but the force of the backwash tore the rope from his hands, taking a fair amount of skin with it, and the three men still in the boat found themselves floating back out again. Karl and Harry leaped into the sea and managed to struggle ashore. They called to Charlie to warn him of the next massive wave rolling in towards him.

Showing considerable coolness amid the chaos, Charlie was determined to get the fire ashore, knowing it was vital to their survival. He made a dive for it with the idea of throwing it ashore with himself close behind it, but as his hands closed around it the lump of earth crumbled into a sizzling mess in the bottom of the boat. Too much water had soaked into it. Their coats, too, were in the bottom of the boat. He just had time to hurl them shore before another wave struck and this one smashed the bow of the little boat clean off. Charlie himself was washed towards the beach where his friends rushed to drag him clear and the wreckage of the boat with him – for somehow Charlie had managed to cling on to the painter. The frame might be destroyed but they needed that canvas!

It took them half an hour, fighting to stay on their feet in the breaking rollers, to raise the boat half out of the water, strip off the canvas and finally get everything safe above the water line. (In fact, they were lucky to make it ashore at all; by good chance, according to the scientists who visited later, they had chosen just about the only spot on the west coast where a landing could have been made).

Looking around, they saw wreckage from the *Dundonald* strewn along the shoreline - masts, yardarms, splintered wood. I fancy there was a touch of irony in Charlie's words as he surveyed the scene.

"*Well, we have reached the Island of Dreams at last, and now I am satisfied.*"

He had been among the most determined to make the attempt, but now he knew only too well that with no fire, no water, no food and no boat they were in deep trouble.

But they had two matches. Karl said they must get a fire going and send a signal back to the other men. When they had done that, they agreed, they would carry the embers with them in a big sod like the one they had used in the boat – and they would make sure it did not go out. Once again Knudsen was showing the leadership and positive outlook that had brought the group through so far.

First, they stripped off their clothes. They were wringing as much water out of them as they could, as naked as the day they were born, when they were startled to hear cracking and rustling in the undergrowth. It sounded like some large creature coming towards them. Nervously they waited until suddenly the head of a seal broke into view. The seal was even more surprised to see them but was unalarmed until it realised they were about to attack it. Then, finding its escape route to the sea cut off it made a charge for them, lunging at Harry who was the nearest, but the men were used to dealing with seals and soon had the makings of their first feed.

It was not easy skinning and cutting up the animal with just one small pocket knife, its blade tied to the handle with string, but Mickey and Harry tackled the job while Charlie and Karl started picking every little piece of rope off the broken frame of the coracle. It was frayed and tarry but it would be needed to build another boat when eventually they returned to Disappointment Island for their mates – after they had found the depot, that is. The optimism that had kept them going so far, motivated them again now.

They decided to tramp as far inland as they could go before making camp for the night. There they would light the fire. They were too exhausted to carry the seal meat with them so they covered it carefully to use the next day. The canvas and the sealskin they took with them to protect them from the cold.

Their aim was to reach the valley that they had been told ran across their way in a north easterly direction up a steep hill. It was then they began to understand how the first party had come to be so scratched and torn. The hill was covered with forest. The rata trees were not tall, not reaching more than twenty feet, but growing so closely together and so thickly entangled with creepers and thorny undergrowth that it was impossible to force a way through them.

There was nothing for it but to return to where they had started and try another track. At one spot there was a cliff, almost bare of bush. It would be easier to try to scale that, they agreed, than to try to penetrate the forest.

They took it slowly, with many pauses for breath for their strength was almost gone. They heaved the canvas and the sealskin with them, passing them up to the man ahead then taking them again while the leaders tackled the next section. Eventually they made it to the top and found themselves at the foot of a wide valley.

There was an eerie silence as they surveyed the steep, bush-covered valley walls rising high above them, waterfalls gushing down the sides. Just as Bob Ellis had described, no birds called, no rustling or sighing came from the trees. Even the roaring of the sea did not reach this high.

They began their tramp along the cliff edge, looking out for the hut they had heard was there. Soon they were being ripped by thorns again. They waded through streams, crawled on hands and knees at times, but the rough hut the first three men had built was there and they reached it at last. The roof was gone but that was soon repaired with long grasses, and there was a creek nearby. All they needed now, they said, was a good fire blazing to warm themselves.

Harry had picked up a piece of dry pitch-pine on the beach and slipped it into his pocket. Now he shaved fine strips off it, piling them into a little heap. They gathered round to protect the match from any draught when it was struck. Karl opened the little tin box.

For a full minute there was utter silence. Not one of them could bring himself to speak. Somehow water had got into the tin and the two matches were soaked through. Somehow they would have to get them dry, but how they were to do that with no sun and no fire they had no idea. There was no answer. Cold and hungry, in their still-damp clothes, they crawled into the hut and tried to sleep. Had they made a dreadful mistake after all, Charlie wondered?

Morning came and with it the need to make decisions. First they must return to the beach for the seal meat they had stashed. They scouted around and found a shorter, easier way than they had taken the day before. They divided the seal meat between the four of them and, each slinging his load over his back, returned to the hut. A break in the clouds allowed a glimmer of sun to shine through. Quickly Charlie laid their two battered matches on the tin lid in the hope that they would dry.

Karl warned him to mind and guard them well and as soon as it clouded over or the mist came down to cover them up again, but as far as Charlie could tell the sun was doing those matches no good at all.

A dense column of smoke was rising from the little island to the west. Mickey groaned at the sight, wishing they could get a bit of that fire over here. Their mates were signalling, but there was no way they could respond.

Harry said at least they could build themselves a better hut.

There was only time that day to clear the ground at a spot further up the creek before night fell and they huddled in the old hut again, stomachs aching with hunger.

"I'm that hungry sure I could eat the soles off me boots, if I had any," said Mickey. His footwear was cobbled from sealskin.

Karl nodded at the meat they had carried up from the beach. There was plenty of food there. The men looked at it glumly. The raw mollymawks had been bad enough; raw seal meat was even worse, but by now they were so desperate they had no choice but to eat it as it was. They cut thin slices, wrapped them in leaves and chewed away. The slimy, fishy taste was revolting, but at least with the worst of their hunger eased they were able to sleep.

The next day passed in much the same way – wet, misty, with an occasional glimpse of sunshine, another meal of raw meat and leaves, another night in the cold hut, talking long into the night for comfort.

Just before daybreak Charlie woke with a start as he heard a sound just outside the hut. It came again, a long, shrill, clear whistle like a signal. The

106

others had heard it too. They rushed outside, but all they could see was shadowy bush, not a soul stirring but themselves. The call came again sounding so close that the hairs on Charlie's neck rose, his superstitious imagination making him wonder if it was *"the spirit of some unhappy castaway who had perished on those lonely forests"* uttering warning cries.

All four of them were unnerved by the eerie sound. Then the first light of dawn crept into the sky and suddenly Harry Walters gave a shaky laugh.

"There he is the little beggar!"

They looked to where he was pointing. A bellbird was perched in the branches of a small tree. It called again, with no fear of the men at all.

This is the only bird Charles Eyre mentions seeing. I doubt if he knew what it was at the time. Again and again the men remarked on the lack of any live creature in the bush, yet there were in fact many species of birds on the islands besides the albatross – a variety of sea birds, gulls, petrels, penguins, ducks as well as domestic animals released by past settlers.

They completed building their new hut but the cold, the damp and the lack of good food was starting to weaken them. Every action was harder work and took longer and they had still made no move to find the supply depot. It seemed like three days wasted, but without food they dared not venture off into the unknown.

A shaft of sun lit the clearing and once again they rushed to expose the matches to its warmth. They wondered if they were dry enough to strike yet, but if they kept them for a year they would be no better than they were then, was Karl's opinion. They must risk it.

They must give it their best go, though, said Harry. He suggested they get a couple of pieces of dry wood and rub them together. When the friction had made them hot they would see if that would light the matches.

It was no easy job to find dry wood, but they found two small lengths and took them into the hut out of the wind. They had saved the shavings Harry had made and these were piled ready to light if the plan worked. They started rubbing it together. On and on they rubbed, taking turns as their hands grew sore and their arms ached.

Karl urged them to keep going. The wood was warm; before long it would get hot. They could not take their eyes off the wood.

Harry asked who was going to strike the match? Not him, cried Charlie. The responsibility was too great. If it did not light he would feel he had failed them all.

No one wanted the job, but finally Harry said he would have a go. With his face set and white he took one of the matches. Mickey continued rubbing. Charlie was shaking as he watched. So much depended on this moment; fire was literally the difference between life and death. Harry struck the match on the hot wood. The men gave a groan of despair as the head came off, leaving a small red streak on the wood. It had been just too soft and damp to burn. Their chances of survival had just been halved.

Harry Walters would have tried the other match, to get it over with but Charlie said no, they could hold out another twenty four hours while it dried more. Karl backed him up so they endured another cold night in the hut.

In his tale Charles Eyre tried to explain the importance of a fire for warmth. He says, "*Perhaps some of my readers may think that the question of food was more important than that of warmth; but they can hardly understand how that awful numbing cold sapped away all our strength. We could struggle on, subsisting on grass and roots, but we could not endure, for any lengthened period, being continually numbed to the bone…. Our blood all seemed frozen; our joints seemed too stiff to move; our limbs felt as if they would give under us when we tried to walk.*"

The next day dawned, fine for once, so their last remaining match was laid out to dry; it was such a tiny thing for their lives to hang on. They sat and watched it, unable to concentrate on anything else, but before an hour had passed the mist began to roll up the creek again. They could wait no longer. Back in the hut they prepared to strike the last match.

Harry instructed Mickey to hold a piece of canvas over the doorway to keep the draught out, so Mickey stood in the entry, arms outstretched holding the canvas in place. He shut out not only any breath of wind that might puff out a tiny flame, but every ray of light as well until the others yelled at him to let in a bit of light, for goodness' sake, before they fell over each other and lost the blessed match! Mickey lowered his arms a few inches until there was enough dim light for them to see what they were doing.

Perhaps the responsibility of trying to strike the very last match was too much for him, but Harry passed the vesta to Karl this time. So while Charlie held one piece of wood steady, Harry rubbed and rubbed with the other getting it as hot as he could. Then Karl leaned forward and struck the last match. There was a crack, a spark. He tried again.

A crack, a fizz. For a fraction of a second a tiny flame shot up bright and clear – then faded away.

The gloom of the hut was nothing to the gloom in the hearts of the four men. Charlie felt he had received a sentence of death. Darkness closed around them as the day drew to an end.

They sat in the darkening hut wondering what to do. At last Mickey said that in his opinion it was not such a bad thing. Now they would have to go on whether they wanted to or not!

Harry Walters had lost all hope. They were going to die, so they might just as well remain where they were and face it without tramping any further through such terrible country, nearly starved to death.

But like Mickey, Charlie always preferred action. Speaking quite sharply, he told Harry to shut up. Mickey was right. They had been messing about there for three days close to starving. If they had made for the depot straight away they might have reached it by now.

Karl had the last word, calming the tension in his steady way. He said they *had* to go on. They could not go back; even if they made another coracle frame, the canvas was too weakened to survive another voyage.

"It's going on, boys, and that is all about it; so let's turn in and wet or fine, we start at daybreak."

CHAPTER ELEVEN

It rained all night, but for once morning dawned bright and fine. They beat their chilled arms across their chests and stamped their feet to get the blood circulating. Then they tied their clothing tightly around them – any buttons had long disappeared – and chewed down a few slices of raw seal meat and leaves. They rolled up the canvas, picked up the sealskin and began to climb.

As they set off up the north east slope of the valley Charlie noticed tracks criss-crossing in several directions. He thought they must be goats, but Mickey looked at them and was sure they were pig tracks -- and pigs meant pork if they could catch them! They reached the head of the valley without sighting a single animal though.

The going became harder. At times they would be floundering through swamps up to their knees in slimy mud then they would be pushing their way through thorny bush that tore at their arms and legs. They limped out of the valley at last, staggering like drunken men.

Karl's face was green. He groaned to Charlie that he was about done for. He thought some of the leaves they had chewed must have been poisonous. With no knowledge of the local vegetation, there was always a risk in eating unfamiliar green-stuff.

Charlie was not feeling too bad so he told Karl to pass over the heavy roll of canvas he was carrying. They would go a bit further and then take a rest. Karl must have been very relieved to pass over his load.

They continued, still bearing north east along the top of the mountain. It was flat up there and they could see for miles. Their own little island looked tiny - a lonely rock in the sea to the west, but north, south, east, all they could see was range upon range of forest-covered hills. They came to more swamp, cut by icy streams, and yet more bush. They heard grunting and squealing and saw a herd of perhaps twenty or so bristly wild pigs, but as soon as the herd sighted the men they fled into the bush.

Auckland Island had been discovered in 1806 by Captain Abraham Bristow. He made a return visit in 1807 and it was then that he released a number of pigs on the island. They bred, increasing in number, but these that the men saw a hundred years later were very wild and difficult to approach. If the idea in releasing them had been to help ship-wrecked seamen, it was a failure for the pigs were far too wily to be caught. They became a pest that destroyed both vegetation and ground-nesting birds.

The sun was casting long shadows by the time they reached another valley which appeared to lead down to a bay. They were still a mile from the sea but just the sight of the water cheered the men. They had walked right across the island.

They were in rata forest again with trees twenty feet tall, carved by the relentless wind into a dense slope down towards the sea so that in places the trunks spread along the ground in a 'most weird and uncanny way' as one of the scientists said later. The ground beneath them was covered with thick moss. Charlie describes how soon there was no room to walk between the trunks so that they found themselves walking on the top of the trees.

"So thick, so dense, and so interwoven were the branches and creepers, that although they gave beneath the feet like a spring mattress, we could walk – or more often roll – over them without falling through."

Charlie did fall through, however, one minute rolling down the sloping branches, the next suddenly plunging through a gap in the canopy to land in a green and gloomy underworld. By the time he had clawed his way out and up again his clothes were all but torn off his back. He was not the only one. They had all fallen more than once by the time they emerged at last at the water's edge where a runnel of fresh water rushed over the rocks into a little bay.

It is possible that they were not walking on the rata trees but on another shrub, suttonia divaracata, which grew up the hillsides to a height of about a metre, or three feet, which was blown by the relentless winds into a dense, tangled mass that a man could walk on.

Whichever it was, they must have been greatly relieved to come out into the open again. Away to the right was a long low spit covered right to the end with the same close forest. To their left another forested headland curved into the sea. They decided to camp there for the night as they were all exhausted but at least they had water.

A bitter little wind sprang up. They shivered. All that wood around them and they couldn't make a fire!

"I wish I had a match," sighed Mickey.

"What's the good of wishing? You might as well wish for a seven course dinner to be served up before you!" Charlie snapped. This was so uncharacteristic of his usual cheerful attitude that it was clear he too was feeling the strain.

Mickey wandered away. Charlie, ashamed of snapping at his friend like that, went after him. Mickey was staring across the stream. Charlie heard him muttering to himself about an object he had noticed across the water. He said it looked to him like a white post, standing all by itself on the other bank.

They called Harry and Karl to come and look. Charlie said it looked just like a white painted signpost – but what was a signpost doing there?

Without wasting another moment Mickey made a direct line for it, straight through the icy cold stream. He was neck-deep in the middle but he plunged on, shaking himself like a dog on the far side. He walked up to the post and stood staring at it until the impatient shouts of the others reached him.

"Mickey! What is it?"

"By all the powers, it is a signpost!"

"Well, what does it say?"

"Four miles to the Provision Depot!" Mickey shouted back joyfully.

Their joy and relief is almost unimaginable. They laughed, they cheered, they danced, but only for a minute. Then they gathered up all the items they had brought with them and rushed to cross the stream to see for themselves.

Soaked to the skin, torn, ragged, bruised and bleeding, they gazed at those wonderful words. Charlie would have sworn he was unable to take another step he was so weary, but now suddenly he was running, scrambling over rocks, leaping streams, wading through the sea if it cut a corner off the way.

They ran out of beach when the deep water came right up to the foot of the cliff and were forced back into the bush, but still they kept to the north eastern direction and as near to the sea as they could. It was dark by now with neither moon nor starlight to help them under the overcast sky. Time and again Charlie found himself blundering into trees or becoming entangled in creepers like a fish in a net. They would have been wiser to rest until daylight, but the thought that at last they were within reach of food, warmth, dry clothing was over-powering. They had to keep going.

Karl warned them to keep calling out as if they got separated now they would never find each other again.

They emerged from the trees on to the beach again and there to their joy was another sign. *Two miles to the provision depot.* They pushed on, but once again were forced to take to the bush when the beach ran out. In their eagerness they forgot about keeping in contact. Charlie realised that for several minutes he had not heard Mickey's Irish accent calling out to him. The other two were up ahead. He called to them to wait.

"Charlie? Where are you?" Harry and Karl called back unable to see him. Charlie kept calling and they followed his echoing calls until they found him, but although all three whistled and coo-eed and shouted Mickey's name there was no answer.

They wondered what to do. Karl was sure he must have heard them – unless he was lying injured somewhere. But Charlie thought of Mickey's cheerful face and the way he had of coming out all right from even the trickiest situations. He was confident that Mickey would get there, especially if there was food and drink ahead. They must trust him as he knew the way as well as they did.

They carried on but it began to seem a very long two miles. Then they caught a glimpse of the sea and soon they were on the beach again. The only problem was, it looked very familiar. When they saw the two mile signpost again they realised they had been going round in circles. They had lost their bearings when they stopped to look for Mickey.

They set off once more, following the winding shore, lit now by a silver gleam as the moon rose. They walked quietly now and carefully, keeping the black wall of trees behind them, listening to the rhythmic shush-shush of the breaking waves. The moonlight touched a tall pole, rising silvery-grey some thirty or forty feet into the air, leaning a little towards the sea. They hurried now and found it was a ship's mast, erected just a little way into the bush.

Charlie reached it first. There was a notice nailed to it.

There was enough moonlight for them to read the notice which stated that the beacons and the depot had been repainted in March 1896 when the store had been replenished. That was nine years ago.

They rounded a bend and there across yet another little bay they saw two white roofs.

"Thank God!" cried Harry. They were all at the end of their strength. *"If only Mickey was with us."*

They made one last effort, crossing a creek that ran into the bay, and came to the small clearing where three sturdy wooden huts had been built.

Suddenly Charlie stopped dead. Then he gave a mighty shout and charged forward, cheering and laughing, for there coming to meet them was Mickey, a ship's biscuit in each hand and his mouth so full he couldn't say a word.

What a mixture of emotions the three men must have felt at that moment. They had found the depot and Mickey Grattan, whom they had feared was lost in the bush, was safe and unharmed. Their first question, of course, was how had he done it? How had he got there before them?

Mickey swallowed his mouthful of biscuit.

"I suppose I smelt these biscuits and me nose led me in a straight line until I came up wid them," he joked.

They rushed to examine the huts. The first was a bunk house, fitted out with bunk beds and a fireplace. The next hut was a storeroom for provisions, while in the third, to their joy, was a wooden boat. They would be able to go back for their shipmates.

The first thing was to get a fire going. They were all wet and cold but Mickey shook his head. He had not been able to find a single match anywhere.

They were sure there must be matches somewhere, but although the clearing was lit by the moon, inside the huts it was too dark to see what the stacks of boxes and packets in the storeroom held. After half an hour searching they gave up. With a couple of large biscuits each they turned in for the night.

The biscuit would have been ship's biscuit or hard tack, a cracker made of flour and water, sometimes a little salt. It was cheap and long-lasting and was also known by a number of other names, some of them giving an idea how hard it was, including pilot bread, cabin bread, tooth dullers, molar breakers, sheet iron and even worm castles because of the weevils that got into it. All the same, it must have tasted amazingly good after months of nothing but meat, 'root', seaweed and leaves. Fortunately their teeth had been strengthened by chewing on the tough mollymawk and seal meat.

CHAPTER TWELVE

Strangely, in spite of his exhaustion, Charlie could not sleep. He was so cut and bruised that every movement was painful. Soaked through, chilled to the bone, he lay on the hard boards of the bunk and shivered and shivered. He had reached that point where he was just too tired to sleep. It was a relief when morning came and they were able to check what stores there were.

As soon as it was light enough, they eagerly opened box after box, calling out to each other in excitement at each new find. Everything was in perfect condition, they discovered, neatly packed in airtight boxes.

Charlie picked up a notice tacked to the lid of a box of biscuit. It read:

N.Z.G.S. Tutanekia, Port Ross,

1-2-07

The ss Tutanekia called here on a visit of inspection and found stores in depot in good order. No sign of human life or wreckage. The vessel leaves here for Carnley Harbour and Campbell Island. Another Government vessel will call here in about six months from date.

T. A. DYKES (Chief Officer)

Charlie folded the paper and stored it in his pocket as a souvenir. He was puzzled. The *Tutaneika* had called there in February, one month before they ran ashore. It said another ship would call in six months from then. That would have been in August but there was no sign that it had been. Surely they must have left a message? Now it was October and even if ships often got delayed, the four men did not think it would be running two months late.

Mickey optimistic as ever, did not want to waste time worrying about that. After all the trouble they had endured reaching the depot, he was not in such a hurry to leave. He wanted to see what was in the boxes.

It was the happiest time the four men had spent since the *Dundonald* went down and almost straight away they found a wooden box that contained two dozen boxes of matches.

Charlie told Mickey to rush off and get a fire started so they could all have a square meal for the first time since the wreck. Mickey promised to cook them an 'elegant' dinner – or they could boil and cook him instead!

Charlie, Karl and Harry opened the boxes. They found six 2lb tins of meat and plenty of biscuits, a dozen thick blankets, a dozen suits of clothing, a dozen shirts, six pairs of underpants and a dozen pairs of boots. They found knives, fishing line, needles, twine, scissors and two big bars of soap. In another box they found an old-fashioned gun, fifty rounds of ammunition, axes, augers, a hammer and nails.

It did not take Mickey long to get a good fire blazing in the bunk house. Over the fireplace was an iron bar with two pots hanging from it on chains. He boiled up tinned meat and biscuits into a thick soup. The smell made their mouths water, but Mickey said it wasn't ready yet so they set to work and cleaned the room out, making up the beds with the blankets they had found. Then they went down to the creek and washed themselves all over with the soap, and cut each other's shaggy hair and trimmed their beards. Properly clean and groomed for the first time in over seven months and dressed in the new clothes, they felt like princes, more than fit to sit down to a good hot dinner – or rather breakfast for it was still only about eight o'clock in the morning.

As they sat around the fire enjoying the hot food they thought of the men still stranded on Disappointment Island. Their first job as soon as they had eaten, they all agreed, must be to overhaul the boat and ready it to fetch them across.

The crossing to Auckland Island had been a gruelling six miles, but now they were on the other side of the island, the eastern side. They were facing a row of over thirty miles up around the northern tip to the small island – unless they could rig up a sail. Once again they were glad they had not abandoned the canvas in spite of its cumbersome weight.

They found a spar in the boatshed that would do for a mast. From the forest they cut a length of wood that would make a gaff, the strut that held the sail out from the mast. Rigging was made by unravelling the three inch thick painter. By evening all was done. Having proper tools to do the work must have seemed like a luxury, halving the time it took to complete the job. They ran the boat down to the water for a trial trip. After steadying her with some rocks for ballast, the boat sailed well. Tomorrow they would go for the others.

They would not be able to bring them all in one run, Karl Knudsen reminded them. One of them had better stay at the depot to leave room for an extra man on the way back.

Charlie suggested that Mickey should stay; they all knew he was the least strong of them. Mickey protested, but not very much. His mates told him to be waiting for them with a good meal when they returned. They would be in need of it!

It could not have been easy to leave the stores of food and clothing and the good beds to tackle the hazardous row back to Disappointment Island, but there was no delay. They knew all too well the dreadful conditions their shipmates were enduring, and set out the next day. They made good time at first with the wind filling the sail so that they skimmed along swiftly. There are a number of small islands off this north eastern tip of Auckland Island, one being Rose Island with, a little further out and somewhat larger, Enderby Island. Here the men met their first problem. The sea between Auckland Island and Rose Island was a seething froth of wild surf and when they tried the passage between Rose and Enderby Islands it was no better. There was no choice but to sail right round the outside of Enderby Island. It was further to go but the only safe way.

As they rounded Enderby Island Charlie gave a cry of surprise. What in the name of goodness, he wondered was that animal on the beach?

Harry said it could not be a seal, it had four legs. Karl said it stood too tall for a pig. When they drew a little closer they could see its horns and realised it was a bull. That was good news – when the tinned meat ran out they could get themselves some beef for where there was one animal there were sure to be others.

Harry pointed out a white painted shed at the edge of the bush. They had spotted the Government Depot built on Enderby Island in 1880. (An earlier hut had been built in 1868, but burned down and replaced in 1880. Also in 1868 two woodhens (wekas) had been released).

They had made about twenty miles, but as they rounded the point, the North West Cape, the wind shifted to dead ahead. There was no way they could make any further progress, either sailing or rowing, against such a wind. Full of frustration, they were forced to turn back. With Karl steering and bailing, Charlie and Harry rowed as hard as they could but by the time they reached the depot again it was nearly dark.

There was Mickey, asleep by the bunk house fire, an empty dish by his side, snoring blissfully. They soon had him awake and bustling about preparing a meal for them before they turned in for the night. The entire day had been used to no avail but tomorrow they would try again.

They were up before daybreak. They ate breakfast, stowed a tin of biscuits in the boat and shut the doors of the sheds securely for this time Mickey was coming with them to share the burden of rowing. It was going to take all the power they could muster to make it around the point.

There was some debate about which route to take. Now they had a fourth man to pull, Charlie thought they should try and run the bar between Rose Island and the mainland. He was thinking of the extra miles it would save. Harry Walters was doubtful, but Karl agreed with Charlie – although as they came closer and closer to the broken water they too began to wonder if they had made the wrong decision. The current was dragging them on to a rocky reef, but it was too late to turn back now. The only question was whether they would get through before they were smashed up against the reef.

Charlie had a moment of surprise among the chaos when the head of a great bull seal rose out of the water in front of them, gave them a stare of amazement and disappeared again. Then they were through, out of the current. Charlie described it as *"a very narrow squeak."* They shot away like a race horse out of the starting gate. Suddenly it was all clear sailing and they were approaching Disappointment Island.

They must have enjoyed the moment immensely when Karl ordered them to unship the mast ready for their approach. They knew they must have been seen, for those on the island, thinking that the boat was a small sealer of some kind, had banked up the fire. Now a great column of smoke was rising from the camp. They would not have signalled if they had believed it was their own shipmates returning.

The four in the boat laughed and joked about how their mates would not recognise them, they looked such respectable fellows now with their hair cut and their new clothes. On the island, the excitement must have been huge. From the boat the tiny figures running to and fro must have appeared like ants in a nest.

When they were within hailing distance Bob Ellis began yelling that there was a landing place on the other side. Charlie and his crew waved, grinning, but did not reply. They were looking forward to seeing the surprise on their faces when they realised who their rescuers were. The boat was close in and the stranded men were right at the water's edge before the truth dawned on them and then a cheer went up that made the rocks ring.

They beached the boat and the questions poured out. Everyone wanted to talk at once.

They had been given up for lost. What had taken them so long? They had spotted a barque to the north the day after the men had left but she had not seen their signals – leastways she never stopped. What was the depot like, they wanted to know? Was there plenty of food there?

The rowers must have been near exhausted, but the joy of those they had left on the island, their relief after they had lost almost all hope, buoyed them up and they answered all the questions. How the castaways must have enjoyed the taste of biscuit.

On the way Charlie, Karl, Harry and Mickey had discussed the best way to transport everyone over to the big island. Of course they still had the little canvas coracle on Disappointment Island, but no one would want to risk crossing in that now they had a proper boat, so they had decided that they would take the strongest men across the six miles of water to the spot where Charlie and his companions had first landed. They agreed not to tell them what they were in for when they got there or none of them would have felt up to tackling it. While that party made the tramp across the island, the boat would return for the weaker members and take them the longer sea route to the depot.

No one could sleep much that night for sheer excitement and soon after midnight they were all up again. All they wanted was to get under way as soon as possible. There would have been no packing to do. There may have been small items carved in spare moments but after hearing of the clothes and tools waiting for them in the huts nothing else would have seemed worth bothering with. In any case they wanted as little to carry as possible, but Charlie warned them to take whatever food they had. They had no idea how tough the trek that awaited them would be and he knew they would find little to eat on the other side until they reached the depot.

Even before the first glimmer of dawn Karl Knudsen, Harry Walters and Santiago Marino pushed out the boat then clambered in themselves with the seven fittest of the crew. They were to bring back the boat after ferrying them across the strait.

Soon after daybreak the boat was back, having made the crossing safely. Karl had pointed out to the seven the direction they must take. Now Charlie, Karl, Harry, Mickey, Santiago, Mr Maclaghlan, John Judge and Alf Finlow could set off. Disappointment Island had been their home for seven months but now they had seen the last of it, and not a day too soon declared Mickey.

It was no easy row at first in an over-loaded boat into a headwind. They unshipped the mast and took to the oars, pulling like madmen when they reached the bar where the water frothed like a boiling cauldron, but they came through it and by four o'clock that afternoon they arrived at the depot.

There was no sign of the trampers. Michael Pul was the first to appear, telling those who greeted him exactly what he thought of them for not warning him what lay ahead. Jack Stewart was next and what he had to say about the tramp was not fit to repeat.

124

Charlie understood; he had been through the same torment just a few days before. The best thing they could do, he knew, was to make sure a good meal was waiting for them as they straggled in during the next two hours.

Eventually everyone was in except young George Ivimey. They had eaten their evening meal and put aside a good plateful for George but still he had not appeared. Growing seriously concerned now Charlie and some of the others went in search of him, whistling and coo-eeing in the bush, but it was growing dark when at last a pitiful figure came staggering into the clearing. George's clothes had been ripped almost entirely off him. He was cut and bruised, one eye blackened and almost closed. It was some time before he was able to tell them how he had lost his way, fallen into creeks, been nearly smothered in a swamp. He had heard the search party calling his name and, although too weak and exhausted to shout back, he had followed the sounds.

I think it was only the severe difficulty of the tramp that caused the men to become separated in that way, taking all their strength so that they did not watch out for stragglers. Fortunately all fifteen of them had made it safely to the depot.

Now all they could do was just make the best of life until a government ship came. Surely that could not be long, they must have hoped?

CHAPTER THIRTEEN

Life was very different now. The weather was starting to improve a little, they had warmth, shelter, new clothing and although the stores of food would not last fifteen hungry men for many weeks, they now had the means to hunt and fish. For a start there was the bull they had seen on Enderby Island. Fish had not been on the menu so far, because due to the seal colony there were very few fish in the waters off shore to be caught.

Now six men took the boat and went to check on the hut on Enderby Island, returning with tins, axes, plates and knives and – best of all – half a tin of tea and some sugar! Who would have believed a cup of tea could taste so good? One of the tins contained a chart of the islands. The chart showed that there were two other depots on Auckland Island besides the Erebus Cove one they had found and on almost every other island there was a boat. The barren little island they had been wrecked on was, they now discovered, called Disappointment Island.

They thought it a most appropriate name since it was the only island without a depot, no supplies and no boat on it. Probably because it was thought no one wrecked on that coast could ever survive to come ashore.

John Judge and Santiago Marino overhauled the old gun they had found. It fired with a mighty kick that sent the marksman staggering until he became used to it, but that was no problem and the next day Michael Pul with the gun and Charlie, Karl, John, Santiago and Herman Querfeldt, all equipped with axes, went hunting on Enderby Island.

There was only one place to land without putting the boat at risk. Close to shore the six men jumped out and ran the boat up the beach. Fifty or more seals lay sunning themselves. They barked and growled aggressively, but it was not seal meat the men were after this time. No doubt they felt they had eaten enough of that to last a lifetime. This time they were after beef.

The cattle had been released on Enderby Island in 1895 by the Moffat family of Invercargill. In 1894 the Auckland Islands had been sub-divided into three areas to be leased out as pastoral, or grazing, runs. The Moffats bought a lease and in 1895 they landed nine Shorthorn cattle and twenty Romney sheep on Enderby Island.

The men soon picked up the trail of the cattle. Enderby is flat, crossed by many creeks and gullies, making the ground swampy and difficult to walk over, but an hour's tramping through the belt of trees that encircled the island brought them to a clearing in the centre.

Michael Pul, the most experienced hunter, warned in a whisper to keep downwind. If the beasts scented them they would be off like a shot.

They crept closer and soon spotted four or five animals grazing along a kind of trench. Michael, keeping low to the ground, edged to the top of the trench to where he could get a good shot. The other five men stayed back in the bush to finish the beast off with their axes if it got past him.

They waited tensely, wondering why he was taking so long. Suddenly a shot rang out and then another. Karl whistled a warning and Santiago yelled, "Look out, Charlie! Look out, man!"

All Charlie had time to do was leap to one side as three monstrous bulls charged straight down upon him. Anything in their way – trees or men alike – went down like matchsticks. He heard John Judge give a yelp of pain as a

127

hoof landed on him as he sprawled on the ground. The beasts were gone and it was no use trying to follow them, but Michael Pul was already on the track of another herd moving nervously along the opposite side of the trench. Sensing danger the animals began to run.

"*Keep up with them! We'll lose them!*" came the shout as Michael took a shot. He hit his mark but it didn't seem to do much more than sting the bull and infuriate it, for it wheeled around and charged its attackers, making straight for Santiago Marino who bravely stood his ground and before the bull could attack the men had brought it down with their axes. It must have been a gory business, but again they were hunting to survive.

Michael had grown up on a farm. He instructed them on how to skin and cut up the carcase into six pieces, one per man. They hefted it back to the beach and there they had to push the boat out into the water before they could load the meat on to it and all the way back they had to bail out the water they were shipping because the boat was so laden.

In the following days they made other hunting expeditions. One cow would last them a week. They brought back other treasures. A canvas sail that they found in the Enderby Island boat house was made into trousers for hunting so as not to ruin their other clothes.

On another island, Ocean Island, not much more than a mile in circumference, they discovered goats and brought back a pair to keep in an enclosure they built. The goats, one brown, one white, became quite tame.

Charlie made many tramping expeditions, exploring as much of the island as he could. One day he set off with just the young cabin boy, Albert Roberts, for company. They walked north, keeping to the beach as much as possible. After some distance they came across two monuments made of brick, each about four feet high. On a stone at the foot of one, he says, was chiselled, "German Expedition, 1870". I think the date was probably *1874*, as according to Edward Kitson, a German expedition landed at Port Ross that year to observe the transit of Venus. They stayed six months.

The transit of Venus was the passing of the planet across the face of the sun, seen as a small black dot. The purpose of observing it, as James Cook had also done in 1769, was to measure the distance from the earth to the sun.

They came across the little cemetery, quite close to the depot, where were buried sailors and others less fortunate than themselves who had not survived. Charlie was obviously moved by the sight; he said, *"It was a sad and solemn thing to stand there in that silent and deserted place,"* looking at the lonely graves. One grave was that of a baby a few months old, buried in 1850, clearly one of the short-lived attempt at a settlement at Hardwicke. No trace was left of the cottages, the church, the cobbled streets of the little settlement.

Another grave was simply marked "Unknown". Next to it was a grave with a board nailed to a tree. The board read:

Erected by the Crew of the
ss Southland over the remains of a man who
had apparently died from starvation and
was buried by the crew of the Flying Scud
3rd Sept., 1865

This last grave was that of John Mahoney, the sole survivor of the ship *Invercauld*. He had scratched his name and the name of his ship on a piece of slate before he died a lonely death in the forest from starvation.

The men were very quiet and thoughtful after seeing these graves. They could only be grateful that the New Zealand government had established the supply depots and equipped them for just such people as themselves or they, too, might by now be dead of hunger and cold.

The best way to shake off such gloomy thoughts was to keep busy. As Charlie said, *"If you had busy thoughts there would be no room for miserable ones, and so we set to work and invented tasks for ourselves."*

It kept them cheerful and prevented quarrels if they were occupied, even if it was at something not particularly useful such as rigging up a flag pole from a mast and making a flag from a piece of old sail. On it they sewed letters cut from a piece of blue cloth they found, spelling out WELCOME with an anchor at each end.

They built a wooden jetty, wading out at low tide to work on it as it grew in length. It was of no practical use, not then, but they enjoyed the activity.

Some of the storage boxes had been lined with zinc. George Ivimey tried his hand at artwork, using a nail and a block of wood to knock holes in a sheet of this soft metal, tapping away until he had the outline of the *Dundonald* with her four masts and all her rigging. Curved around the top he put the words DUNDONALD WRECKED MARCH 17 1907 Down the left side he added 12 DROWNED, 16 SURVIVED, MATE PERISHED FROM EXPOSURE. Along the bottom he put his name – G. IVIMEY SOUTHAMPTON

Pleased with the result, he also hammered out a distress message which he nailed to a piece of wood. He fixed a little sail to it and set it adrift on the sea. People found messages in bottles; why shouldn't they find his piece of wood? It was found later, washed up on Campbell Island and given to Albert Roberts who later gave it to the Canterbury Museum.

When the day was over and the darkness closed in, they gathered in the bunk house, singing, telling yarns and drinking 'coffee' made from biscuit that had been ground into a powder and burnt! Well, it was hot and brown and tasted of something, thought Charlie, even if he couldn't decide exactly what. It was their *"one and only luxury"*.

Charlie was a smoker. He says they tried smoking, making themselves pipes by carving the bowls out of wood and using bird bones (which are hollow) as the stems. For tobacco they shredded rope-yarn *"but as it was full of tar, a very few whiffs were enough to satisfy us, and convince us that it was not the sort of tobacco suited to our constitutions, so we gave it up entirely."*

They had survived – but always, every day, they kept watch for the ship that surely must come soon.

CHAPTER FOURTEEN

They kept themselves busy. Hunting, exploring the closer parts of the island, keeping the huts and the boat in good order, cooking, whittling away at pieces of wood; there was always something to do. Morale was good. The certainty that, even if they had a long wait, eventually a Government ship would come to check on the supply depot must have kept them cheerful.

It was the middle of November, early in the morning on Friday 15 November by Bob Ellis's reckoning, that Karl Knudsen and another man went down to the beach to ready the boat for a hunting expedition. It was Karl's shrill whistle that woke Charlie. He sat up in his bunk.

"That's Knudsen. What on earth's the matter with him?"

"Will you hush now?" said Mickey. *"What's that they're shouting?"*

Then they heard, *"A ship! A ship!"* They rushed outside, just as they were, and at the sight of the ship the men went wild. This was no passing vessel that might not see their signals. This ship was making directly for the island. They did not stop to eat breakfast but as it drew closer they rushed back to put on their good clothes – just as if we were receiving visitors and wanted to make a good impression, Charlie thought – while a boat was lowered from the *Hinemoa* and rowed ashore. Charlie never forgot the surprise on the faces of those on board when they were greeted by fifteen castaways, dancing with joy on the beach, throwing their hats in the air and cheering like lunatics! There was surprise, too, at the sturdy jetty they had constructed.

The Government Survey Ship *Hinemoa's* arrival was a stroke of pure luck for this was not a routine check on the depot, she was on a Sub-Antarctic scientific expedition, to the islands in that area. The captain, Captain Bollons, explained that she would not be returning to New Zealand for another two weeks at least and there was no room to take fifteen extra men on board for that long so they would have to wait until the ship had completed her survey and was on the way home. Then they would come back and take them off, back to New Zealand he promised.

They were disappointed, of course, protesting that they did not care where they slept – on deck, anywhere – but the captain said it simply was not possible. He would leave them extra provisions for two weeks – meat, biscuits, tea, sugar – and be back. They had been on Auckland Island for two months and some supplies were running low by then, although they were in no danger of starvation since they were able to hunt. They had long been out of tea and sugar. The men on board the *Hinemoa* were, in fact, surprised at how healthy they were after being stranded for eight months.

Charles Eyre, Karl Knudsen, Harry Walters, Jack Stewart and the First Mate Mr MacLaghlan went out in their own boat to the *Hinemoa* to collect the provisions. The rail was lined with curious faces. Their own faces, they knew, were still gaunt and yellow, their hair and beards long although now they were able to trim and comb them so they did not look quite as wild as they once had. At least their teeth, once stained brown from chewing tobacco, were now clean and white, a side effect from chewing 'root' and having no tobacco. On board they were almost overwhelmed by all the questions thrown at them.

The captain's excuse that he had no room for extra people aboard was true, they saw. The ship was, indeed, already crowded with a party of eleven scientists and a gang of four shearers. There was nothing for it but to wait on their island until the ship picked them up on her way home. It wasn't so bad with the extra provisions, knowing that at last they had been found and would not be forgotten.

The *Hinemoa* was on what was described as a Philosophical Expedition, studying and collecting the plants and wildlife of the sub-Antarctic islands, including twelve Auckland Island flightless ducks which were later released on Kapiti Island, and making magnetic observations.

As they prepared to climb down the rope ladder into their now heavily laden boat, one of the scientists, *"a well-dressed gentleman"* took Charlie's arm and drew him aside. He explained he was one of the party stopping off at Campbell island. They were on a scientific expedition. They would be there about a week, camping and were in need of a cook. He asked Charlie how he felt about taking the job. Would he do it?

Charlie hesitated. He said he was not what you would call a real cook.

Mr MacLaghlan had overheard the conversation and put in a good word, saying that of course he could cook as well as any of them after all those months on the island. Charlie thought about it. If he stayed on the island he would have nothing to do but laze around waiting for the *Hinemoa* to return. There would be no need to hunt for they had plenty of supplies now and he liked to keep busy. He knew there would plenty of hard work to be done, but as he said, *"I was going to fresh scenes and pastures new and that has always been the delight of my life; a roamer I have been, and a roamer I shall be, I suppose, to the end of the chapter."*

He agreed to do it.

Charlie stayed aboard the *Hinemoa* when it sailed on its way to drop the scientists and shearers off at Campbell Island.

He found it strange to be among new people; to talk to well-educated men after hearing nothing but sailor's slang and broken English for so long. The *Hinemoa* had been built as a yacht and the salon was very elegant compared to the rough quarters of a working ship. At first Charlie felt very out of place. He seemed to have forgotten all about what he called the decencies of civilised life, *"so that a knife and fork seemed as something new to me, and a white tablecloth a thing to be terribly frightened of."* He wished the deck would open and he could sink out of sight.

The scientists were kind to him and easy going and soon he was comfortable with them. He admits he was never a shy person by nature and soon got over any awkwardness.

They arrived on Campbell Island the next day and it was then he learned that they had actually been found on Saturday 16 November – Bob Ellis had been just one day out, carrying an account of the days in his head. They were to be on the island for a week. Only two men lived on Campbell Island, shepherds looking after a number of sheep for their New Zealand owner. The four shearers had come to join them for three months after which a ship would call to take them and the wool clip home.

Charlie's first job was to make tea, with water so strong and brown from the peat the water ran through that everyone thought he had poisoned them. The taste certainly took some getting used to. Besides tea, he cooked cocoa, porridge, eggs, bacon and potatoes – and that was just breakfast. Then there were good, hot dinners. He was kept busy, but his months of practice on the islands stood him in good stead.

The scientists included botanists, geologists, biologists and the magnetic observers that Charlie shared a tent with. One of them told how Charlie woke them in the morning with the words, *"Now gently rise and shine."*

One of the scientists was Edward Kidson. He kept a diary of events. When his wife edited and published it years later in the 1940s, it was suggested that the ship's master, Captain Bollons, wanted to check out the truthfulness of the story the castaways had told him. It was not unheard of for a crew to mutiny and dispose of their officers. He felt that Charlie, a naturally talkative character, would be the most likely to let slip any facts that did not match the original account. He had been invited to go along as cook to separate him from the others. Needless to say, the story proved to be true in every respect and all suspicion was banished.

Charlie shared a tent with three of the scientists, all young like himself, and one day they took him with them to see a bit of the island while they photographed the wildlife. On another tramp Charlie found some purple heather growing just as it did in the highlands of Scotland. It was time he was going home, he thought, as he tucked a sprig into his pocket as a souvenir.

The day came for the *Hinemoa* to return to pick up the castaways. The scientists packed up their equipment and, with Charlie, went aboard. After a stop at Carnley Harbour in the south of Auckland Island, where the captain took soundings to mark on the chart, they carried on to Norman's Inlet on the east coast where they spent the night.

Before they left they painted the supply depot there. Charlie wondered if it would one day be the saving of another crew like that of the *Dundonald*. Then they steamed on north towards Port Ross to pick up Charlie's mates. The men had stayed near camp, sheltering from the gales and rain that had returned after the spell of fine weather and watching out for the ship, but it was 25 November, three days after she had been expected, that she arrived.

The *Hinemoa* stayed there for the night, but before they departed finally for New Zealand, there was one last visit to be made. They left at daybreak for Disappointment Island. They steamed right around the island

and saw the place where the *Dundonald* was wrecked, and the steep hill rising behind it. It seemed incredible that anyone had reached the shore alive.

The people from the *Hinemoa* were amazed to see the old dwelling huts and cook houses, eighteen of them in all. The framework of the old canvas boat was there, the bone needles, the mollymawk skin blankets, the meat hooks of twisted wood, all the many things they had made to make life possible on the island. The place was littered and frankly rather smelly. The scientists said the framework of the coracle ought to be preserved and put in one of the museums so the men from the *Dundonald* gave it them immediately for the Canterbury Museum, in Christchurch, along with various other items.

While the scientists took numerous photographs, Mr MacLaghlan, Karl Knudsen, Michael Pul and another man had one special task to perform. They went to fetch the body of First Mate Jabez Peters from its rough grave so that it could be given a decent burial at Port Ross. It was not a pleasant job, but it was the least they could do for him, they all agreed.

They returned to Ross Harbour and there, in the Hardwicke cemetery, they held a simple ceremony for Mr Peters and erected a wooden cross, made by George Ivimey, at the head of his new grave so that all who saw it would know who lay there. Then they went back to the ship, ate their dinners and went to bed.

The next day, 29 November, after more than eight long months as castaways, the crew of the *Dundonald* set sail at last for Bluff, in the very south of New Zealand. They arrived in Bluff about four o'clock on Saturday afternoon on the last day of November.

On the way Charlie had mentioned that he wanted to send a cable to his family as soon as possible, to let them know he was alive, so the scientists he had cooked for on Campbell Island found the money and as soon as the *Hinemoa* had docked one of them went with Charlie to the Post Office and helped him send a message. One word said it all:

"*Eyre, Elsie Road, East Dulwich. Rescued – Charlie.*"

CHAPTER FIFTEEN

The arrival of the castaways in Bluff caused a sensation. The *Dundonald* had been officially listed as missing on Lloyd's Shipping Register and all the crew presumed drowned. Lloyd's Register was started in 1760 as a list of ships to give insurers and merchants an idea of the condition of the vessels they insured or chartered. The ships were graded, both hulls and fittings, and stayed on the Register until they were sunk, wrecked, hulked or scrapped.

The families of the *Dundonald* crew must surely have given up all hope of ever seeing their menfolk again. When the good news was telegraphed back to Britain I can only imagine the joy of those who heard their loved ones were still alive and the grief of those whose loss was confirmed.

In New Zealand the excitement was huge. The Otago Witness, a weekly newspaper, reported on Wednesday 4 December that *"Their arrival and the story of their adventures aroused great interest in the Bluff, and also in Invercargill, hundreds of townspeople going to the port by this afternoon's train to hear the story for themselves and see the rude boat in which the castaways trusted their lives in getting from Disappointment to Auckland Island."*

The newspaper gave a detailed account of the wreck and listed the names, ages and home towns or countries of those lost, along with the names of the men who had survived, as told to 'Our Own Correspondent' in Invercargill on 1 December by Karl Knudsen. This was followed by more details from *'Our Special Correspondent'* in Bluff who interviewed Charles Eyre, *'an able seaman, aged 21'* on 30 November. Oddly, the only name left out of both articles was that of the First Mate, Jabez Peters, although his death was mentioned and he was described as an *'older man'*.

The paper went on to say, *"On Saturday night steps were taken to raise some money for the unfortunate men, and today the Bluff Band gave an open air concert on the wharf in their aid and a fair sum was raised. At present the men are lodged at Whealler's Hotel and are fairly well clad...."*

The disaster was described as *"one of the most remarkable of the many wrecks that have taken place on the rock-bound coasts of the inhospitable Auckland Islands. Much heroism was displayed by the men in assisting each other to land, and a great deal of resourcefulness and energy was afterwards shown by them in maintaining life on an inclement little island and afterwards in finding their way to the provision depot at Auckland Island."*

It was the admiration felt by people for the resourcefulness of the castaways and the determined efforts they had made to help themselves, as much as sympathy for what they had gone through, that moved the Southlanders to help them. The Mayor of Invercargill started a fund in their aid. He sent a telegram to the Shipwreck Relief Society asking if they would head the list with a donation of £10 or whatever sum they wished.

The Mayor said in his telegram that *"the men are all right and cared for. I am, however, asking the citizens to subscribe to a fund to divide amongst the surviving men, not that they need it very much, because they are in a good country, and will be able to get work; but more as an expression of our sympathy with their sufferings and admiration for their indomitable fight for life."*

At a meeting of the Shipwreck Relief Society the committee voted to give each man £2 with an additional £1 for each of the officers, to be given to the men as pocket money. They felt that the small amount was justified because the citizens of Invercargill were also donating to the relief fund.

The men truly were well looked after. Charles Eyre said, "Nothing seemed too much for them to do for us. One gentleman, named Macky, gave me a perfect new suit of clothes and boots, and everything else that I needed to make me look respectable. Mr Hutton took the whole of us to a clothiers, where he fitted us all out."

Officials from the Board of Trade interviewed the men, making them an allowance and arranging for their transport home. It may be that some of them did not choose to go back – we do not know what happened to most of them – but Charlie accepted the offer of a passage back to London. He was actually on his way to Bluff station on Saturday 7 December, when he was approached by the chief officer of a steamer named the *Whakatane* who asked him if would like to sign on. He had been asked by the same man before and refused.

But, as he says, "I don't know what possessed me. Anyone might have said that I had surely had enough of seafaring for a time, but I told myself that as the vessel was going to London, I might as well work my passage home as go as passenger and so I became one of the crew..."

He was not the only one; Mickey Gratton, George Ivimey and Herman Querfeldt had signed on, too. They sailed from Lyttleton on 29 December, finally bound for home. Charlie recounts his voyage home, via Cape Horn, with various ports of call on the way. He tells of the delays and hold-ups, the frustrating slowness of berthing when they were so near to home and how late it was before they were finally moored. They decided it was too late to try to get home that night. He was below, having a last farewell yarn with his friends from the *Dundonald*, when he was called to come up on deck.

He muttered and growled a bit about always something to be done, but up he went. There, come aboard, was his father and with him Charlie's brother, his two sisters and his brother-in-law. He could not find the words to describe that reunion to Rev Escott-Inman, but he tells how slow the ride seemed in the horse-drawn cabs – they needed two – through the streets of London and how good it was to be back.

"The mud, and the cabs, and the buses, and the crowd, and the gas glaring in the shops, it was all part of a beautiful picture...." Best of all was home and, waiting for him, his mother.

THE END

AUTHOR'S NOTE

I called this story *Fifty South* because the latitude of the Auckland Islands is 50 degrees 40 minutes south of the Equator. This sub-Antarctic latitude was the single most influential circumstance that made their ordeal so terrible and their survival so extraordinary. The weather is rarely fine. The Captain of the *Hinemoa* said, when they called at Disappointment Island, *"The combination of a clear sky, windless day and smooth sea, is never found in these latitudes, and we were fortunate therefore in getting two of them – a smooth sea and a windless day. It was raining heavily, but this was a minor evil."* If they had been wrecked in the short summer months they would probably have seen a mass of brightly coloured flowers.

I have used the spelling of the names as given by Charles Eyre to Rev. Escott-Inman. Those in the newspapers vary, but I felt that overall Charles Eyre's were as likely to be correct as any other.

The government supply depots were maintained until 1929. After that time the servicing of them was discontinued. By then virtually all commercial shipping was equipped with radio so in the event of an emergency able to signal their position – as the *Titanic* did in 1912, just five years after the *Dundonald* went down. In 1934 the whole of the Auckland Islands was protected as a nature reserve. During World War Two there were five coastwatcher stations on the islands. In 1993 they were declared a marine mammal sanctuary and in 2003 became the Motu Maha Reserve. Most recently, 2014, a proposal has been put forward to establish a new research station named after Sir Peter Blake, on the east coast of the main island, to carry out research into climate change. It will be pest free, all pigs, cats and mice eradicated.